21st Century Common Sense

by

Felton Williamson, Jr.

authorHOUSE®

AuthorHouse™
1663 Liberty Drive
Bloomington, IN 47403
www.authorhouse.com
Phone: 1-800-839-8640

First published by AuthorHouse 10/14/2009

ISBN: 978-1-4490-3282-1 (e)
ISBN: 978-1-4490-3280-7 (sc)
ISBN: 978-1-4490-3281-4 (hc)

Library of Congress Control Number: 2009910907

Printed in the United States of America
Bloomington, Indiana

This book is printed on acid-free paper.

"THESE ARE THE TIMES THAT TRY MEN'S SOULS"

THOMAS PAINE, 1776

FOREWORD

This book may be the last act of an old man, trying to save his country from a totalitarian dictatorship.

Years of deterioration of America's basic education has resulted in a majority of our citizens' failure to understand individual freedom and the role that individual freedom plays in the creation of wealth and prosperity. This book provides the historic proof that creation of wealth and your prosperity was impossible until the "divine rights of the King" was discarded in favor of individual freedom. Individual freedom was the indispensible ingredient in the "Industrial Revolution" and the driving force of the American Revolution.

The "WANNABE PEERS" mounted a counterattack to the American Revolution in the late 19th Century. The effect of that counterattack on individual freedom has been devastating. A great deal of research was necessary to be able to present the Effects of this "counter attack" on our individual freedom.

The extensive research is detailed in the Bibliography (9 pages). Most of the research was done on the internet and the website addresses are listed in the bibliography. However, anyone interested in visiting those websites may find it easier to go to the author's website, http://commonsense21c.com/, click on the "bibliography" link and visit any of the listed websites by clicking on the website address in the bibliography.

The websites are listed because of the facts contained there, not the analysis and conclusions of those facts. The conclusions (on the research website) do not always agree with the conclusions made in this book. Of course you are free to decide whose interpretation of the facts is correct.

The purpose of the book is to try to rewrite Mr. Paine's "COMMON SENSE" as he would write it today, with the advantage of over 200 years of history unavailable to him in 1776. That is quite an ambition for a senile old man. Was I successful? Please email your comments, along with the proof of any disagreements or fallacies you find to tobywil3@yahoo.com. After all, I may be old but I am not too old to learn.

To establish a time frame, this book was started on September 8, 2008 and the manuscript was completed on September 7, 2009.

I have to thank to my soul mate of over 50 years, B. Francine Williamson, and our son Felton III (aka Lou) for their encouragement, comments and proof reading the manuscript. Without their help and encouragement there would be no book and you would have saved a few bucks.

GOD BLESS AMERICA!

TABLE OF CONTENTS

PAGE

CHAPTER 1 21ST CENTURY
"COMMON SENSE"   1

CHAPTER 2 WEALTH   26

CHAPTER 3 ECONOMIC SYSTEMS   59

CHAPTER 4 20TH CENTURY
DICTATORS   82

CHAPTER 5 "WANNABE PEERS"
STRATEGY & TACTICS   107

CHAPTER 6 "WANNABE
PEERS" SUCCESSES   136

CHAPTER 7 SHERMAN
ANTITRUST ACT   143

CHAPTER 8 THE BUREAUCRACY-ICC   164

CHAPTER 9 INFLATION AND
MANIPULATION OF THE DOLLAR   182

CHAPTER 10 EARMARKS   194

CHAPTER 11 THE INCOME TAX   200

CHAPTER 12 THE WAY BACK   211

BIBLIOGRAPHY   235

CHAPTER ONE

"21ˢᵀ CENTURY COMMON SENSE"

Over two hundred years have passed since we won our freedom from KING GEORGE III. We are again standing on "LEXINGTON GREEN[25]" with our freedom in peril, just as it was when the "MINUTEMEN" faced the British Regulars on the fateful day of April 19, 1775; the day the "shot heard around the world" started the American Revolution.

The threat is no longer the **"DIVINE RIGHT OF KINGS"**[30] enforced by KING GEORGE III and his "PEERS". Today the danger is accepting the "WANNABE PEERS'" promise of security and unearned wealth.

In 1776, the Colonies stood at the crossroads between FREEDOM and the TYRANNY of KING GEORGE III. On January 10, 1776, faced with this choice of freedom or tyranny, Thomas Paine[47] published the pamphlet "COMMON SENSE"[47]. The pamphlet was America's first and most important bestselling book. Thomas Paine's "COMMON SENSE" inspired the Colonists to choose freedom and prosperity.

For over 100 years the "WANNABE PEERS" (politicians lusting after the power and prestige enjoyed by KING GEORGE III'S "PEERS") have used false promises of security and unearned wealth to regain that power and prestige. The "WANNABE PEERS'" campaign has

1

been very successful. Our "FOUNDING FATHERS" would be appalled at the loss of freedom and the power wielded by the bureaucrats and "WANNABE PEERS" of today.

Instead of the British Regulars that advanced on "LEXINGTON GREEN", we are faced with hordes of bureaucrats. Make no mistake about it; the bureaucrat's weapons are just as effective against you as the British Regular's muskets were against the original MINUTEMEN.

The "WANNABE PEERS" program has created a system that is almost as oppressive as the system that caused the original Minutemen to rebel. Unless the present trend is reversed, we will soon live under the tyranny of a totalitarian government.

The choice must be made now; it will soon be too late. Will you choose the freedom created by the "FOUNDING FATHERS" or will you be seduced by the "WANNABE PEERS'" false promises of security and unearned wealth?

In Thomas Paine's time, the prevailing form of government was the "KINGDOM". Though nomenclature varied with the location, there was little difference between the "KINGDOMS". Some "KINGDOMS", such as England, placed some restrictions on the absolute power of the "KING". Any restrictions on the absolute power of the "KING" increased individual freedom and the most prosperous of these "KINGDOMS" were those with the most individual freedom. The "KINGDOM" form of government was considered normal and was accepted by the "COMMONS"; few recognized that there was an alternative. Mr. Paine's "COMMON SENSE" provided that alternative.

"COMMON SENSE" was a clear, logical, easily understood and irrefutable defense of individual freedom. Eloquent and inspiring, Mr. Paine's condemnation of England's near "Totalitarian" KINGDOM and the promotion of individual liberty inspired the Colonists to fight and win independence.

The arguments in "COMMON SENSE" are as valid today as they were when the pamphlet was written over 200 years ago and the "KINGDOM" form of government has been thoroughly discredited. Today, few dare to openly advocate the "KINGDOM" form of government.

Once free of tyranny, the Colonists established a government that guaranteed individual freedom (for citizens) including the right to create and enjoy wealth. Perhaps the only flaw was denying citizenship to some residents. The result was over 200 years of prosperity and technological achievement that is unequalled in the history of the world. In less than 200 years, the state of the art of transportation changed from horses and sailing ships to supersonic aircraft, nuclear submarines and automobiles travelling on super highways. Innovation, featuring the use of mechanical energy to replace "muscle power", provided huge increases in individual productivity. The reduction in labor and resources required to produce the necessities of life freed those resources to produce luxuries for the masses. Increases in individual productivity created prosperity undreamed of when our Constitution was adopted. Luxuries, unheard of in KING GEORGE III's day, became commonplace. The standard of living of each generation improved and that increasing prosperity continued into the Twenty-First Century.

CHAPTER ONE

When America won independence, the source of power changed from the "KING" to the ballot box. With the change in the source of power, a new class of citizen emerged - the "WANNABE PEERS". The "WANNABE PEERS" lusted after the power and prestige that the British "PEERS" had enjoyed under KING GEORGE III.

"WANNABE PEERS" wanted to use the government's monopoly on force to control the "COMMONS" (creators of wealth) and punish those who resisted their benevolent coercion.

The "WANNABE PEERS" realized that new strategic and tactical initiatives would be required to regain the power that the British "PEERS" enjoyed under the "KING".

The "WANNABE PEERS" devised tactics and strategy to use the ballot box to regain their lost power. Realizing that their natural constituency was the desperate and poverty stricken, the "WANNABE PEERS" knew that general prosperity and economic stability were not in their best interest. Both Hitler and Mussolini required severe economic crises to achieve their coup.

The "WANNABE PEERS" would claim the moral "high ground" and proclaim that the purpose of their agenda was to aid the unfortunate, provide security, improve the environment (added later), correct social injustices, and prevent exploitation of the consumer by the producer. However, the **real** purpose of their agenda was to regain the power and prestige possessed by KING GOERGE III's "PEERS".

Prosperity is the most formidable obstacle to the "WANNABE PEERS'" increasing their power. Even though the "WANNABE PEERS" claim to aid the "unfortunate", almost every item in their agenda destroys wealth. The proof of this assumption is contained in the evaluation of five of the "WANNABE PEERS" "showcase programs" (see chapters 7, 8, 9, 10, and 11). The destruction of wealth has the greatest effect on the standard of living of the "unfortunate" and forces more people below the poverty level. Pushing more of the population into poverty will increase "WANNABE PEERS'" constituency.

The "common enemy" is a necessity for those who would usurp your liberty and the "WANNABE PEERS" selected the "RICH" (the creator of wealth and Mr. Paine's "COMMONS") as the common enemy. Hitler's enemies were the Jews and Communists, Mussolini's enemies were the Communists and Socialists. The "WANNABE PEERS'" "preponderance of propaganda" campaign would dwell on the positive results they promised for their agenda and ignore the negative results that would actually occur.

The "WANNABE PEERS" were able to make very little progress until the late 19TH Century. The "WANNABE PEERS" first big success was the Sherman Antitrust act[24], a non objective law that could be applied against any successful "COMMONS", (creators of wealth). The Sherman Antitrust Act was enacted in 1890. The second hundred years rewarded the "WANNABE PEERS" with compounding successes. The "WANNABE PEERS" enhanced their power and are very close to completely dismantling the great economic engine that the "FOUNDING FATHERS" created. America's first "retro-generation" will soon be a reality. When the "standard of living" declines for a generation, that generation is a "retro generation". We may already be members of the first American "retro-generation.

CHAPTER ONE

A detailed analysis of the successes of the "WANNABE PEERS'" agenda and the results of those successes are presented later. Briefly, the "WANNABE PEERS" successes are:

- Earmarks that in 2008 removed $16.5 billion dollars from the economy.
- Meddling in the relationship between the employer and employee has virtually bankrupted the American automobile industry, increased everyone's cost of living (inflation) and resulted in government enforced racial discrimination. The meddling has allowed the "WANNABE PEERS" to obtain political support for the favors provided to the "PAWNS" (special interests).
- Rules and regulations restricting the harvesting of natural resources have made us dependent on those hostile to freedom for our energy, resulting in the squandering of our wealth and preventing creation of wealth in our country.
- An Income Tax Code too complicated to understand or comply with. It has the capacity to make anyone a criminal, requiring only a close enough investigation to find the non-compliance. This has huge potential to stifle political dissent.
- Taxing productivity (income tax) can only have the effect of limiting the creation of wealth.
- Non objective antitrust laws that are interpreted by political expediency and change with the judge and political pressure. These laws punish productivity, reward mediocrity and stifle innovation.

- Creating a bureaucracy that acts as police, prosecutor, judge, and jury. Enforcing its rules and regulations by reversing the basic tenet of our law that one is innocent until proven guilty. (Examples? The IRS and EPA come to mind. The bureaucracy has a huge potential to silence political dissent).
- Rules and regulations involving health care and drugs that have driven the cost of health care to the ridiculous extreme by catering to special interests.
- A justice system that allows for years of incarceration (innocent until proven guilty?) prior to trial and requires one to expend one's life savings for defense. The reward for innocence? Possibly an apology and loss of one's life savings.
- Destruction of the Constitution by appointing judges that legislate from the bench, giving the "WANNABE PEERS" the power to create laws that could not be passed by the Legislature.
- Bureaucracies requiring "environmental impact statements" that delay projects for years and increase the cost of innovation, preventing the creation of wealth. The same bureaucracy has the power to create and enforce new rules and regulations that wreak havoc on the economy with no regard for the consequences of their actions.
- Behavior control laws that create victimless crimes and "controlled substance" laws that are no more effective than the "prohibition laws" of the early Twentieth Century. The laws provide a source of income for the criminal element,

dislocate the economy and fail to protect the public from erratic behavior caused by the use of dangerous drugs.

The affects of the success of the "WANNABE PEERS'" agenda is very close to creating the economic crisis that is required to achieve the coup. Today, we are all standing on the 21ST Century "Lexington Green"[25] and unless we take immediate action, KING GEORGE III and his henchman "PEERS" will have the last laugh.

The "WANNABE PEERS" tell us we should surrender our freedom (and our prosperity) for the promise of security and unearned wealth. BENJAMIN FRANKLIN'S[19] eloquent quote "**THEY WHO WOULD GIVE UP AN ESSENTIAL LIBERTY FOR TEMPORARY SECURITY, DESERVE NEITHER LIBERTY OR SECURITY**" would seem to settle the question of swapping freedom for security.

The use of the government to provide advantage of one citizen over another is a fleeting proposition that shifts with the political fortunes resulting in the loss of freedom for all concerned and only enhances the power of the "WANNABE PEERS". Mr. Paine could never have conceived of a people, once free, surrendering their liberty for promises of security, unearned wealth or political advantage over their neighbor.

Mr. Paine divided the citizens of England into three Classes:

- The "KING"
- The "PEERS"
- The "COMMONS"

Of course, the "KING" is not a factor in America now, but the "KINGS" (goes by many names) still control much of the world. The "PEERS", or aristocrats, who held the position

8

of authority at the "KING'S" pleasure, are long gone. Their philosophical descendants have been replaced by politicians, "WANNABE PEERS", using the ballot box to try to obtain the power and prestige formally bestowed by KING GEORGE III on his "PEERS".

To update Mr. Paine's citizens list to the Twenty-First Century, it is necessary to add one Class, the "PAWNS". This terminology will be used throughout this book. The use of the common labels, Communist, Socialist, Fascist, "Conservatives" and "Liberals" are just part of the confusion. All those common labels are used to describe politicians who covet your freedom. Ayn Rand, perhaps history's greatest champion of Capitalism, was asked if she were a Conservative. "No" was her answer. She said she was a "radical for Capitalism", that there was nothing left to conserve. The fallacy that Communism, Socialism and Fascism were at different ends of the political spectrum was used very successfully by both Hitler and Mussolini in their quest for power. (See CHAPTER 4) The political spectrum consists of INDIVIDUAL FREEDOM on the extreme right and the various forms of slavery (Communism, Socialism and Fascism) on the extreme left. The mixed economy spans the area between FREEDOM and SLAVERY. The only difference between Communism, Socialism and Fascism is the rhetoric, the arguments and personality of the Dictator.

The "KING" had virtually unlimited power and delegated that power to the "PEERS" for the oppression of the "COMMONS" (producers). The wealth extracted by the oppression of the "COMMONS" maintained the "PEERS" and the

"KING" in what passed for luxury in the pre-industrial revolution world. Although in 1776 England, his power was theoretically limited, the "KING" could manipulate the system to achieve his purpose.

In Mr. Paine's day, the "PEERS" status was determined by birth and maintained at the pleasure of the "KING". "PEERS" controlled considerable wealth and power so they were easy to identify. There was little or no movement between classes. Not so today. **Any ambitious political psychopath can become a "WANNABE PEER".**

The post-revolution "WANNABE PEERS" are the leaders of the groups that seek to control and/or exploit the individual by using the government's monopoly on force. The "WANNABE PEERS" are divided into three groups:

The "POWER SEEKING WANNABE PEERS" are those seeking power for power's sake. They want to upgrade themselves into the "KINGS" Class. Hitler is an excellent example of this most dangerous type of "WANNABE PEER". Some may even believe their own propaganda and see themselves as the "savior of the masses".

"ECONOMIC WANNABE PEERS" try to use the power of the Government to achieve financial advantage. The confiscation of private property and subsequently awarding the property to the "ECONOMIC WANNABE PEERS" for "economic development" is an excellent example of the successful campaigns by the "ECONOMIC WANNABE PEERS". Another common objective of the "ECONOMIC WANNABE PEERS" is to seek to use the power of the government to maintain the "status quo" when innovation threatens to cause them economic damage.

"BEHAVIOR CONTROL WANNABE PEERS" seeking to use the power of the Government to force their ideas (a limited agenda) on the individual. If they are successful, they will try to expand their agenda. The Eighteenth Amendment, "Prohibition", is an example of their success.

Both the "ECONOMIC WANNABE PEERS" and the "BEHAVIOR CONTROL WANNABE PEERS" might be considered "PAWNS" because they are the "special interest" the "POWER SEEKING WANNABE PEERS" exploit to obtain power.

Modern "WANNABE PEERS" are much more subtle and devious than Mr. Paine's "PEERS". Heredity no longer defines one as a "PEER". Today, the "WANNABE PEERS" are defined by their actions and the identity as a "WANNABE PEER" is carefully hidden even after obtaining power. For the "WANNABE PEERS", the end justifies the means and they will use any form of deception to obtain power. After all, no one will surrender their liberty if they know what they are doing. To use the ballot box as a source of power, the "WANNABE PEERS" created the new class, the "PAWNS".

The "PAWNS" are those deceived by the "WANNABE PEERS" and believe that the "WANNABE PEERS" will provide access to the "COMMONS'" property, or give them a competitive advantage or the means to force their will on the "COMMONS". The "PAWNS" don't realize that they too are surrendering their freedom.

In 1776 England, the "COMMONS" were the real creators of wealth. It was the "COMMONS" who actually produced the food, built the ships and produced the wealth required for society to exist. The "COMMONS" lived on the crumbs they were able to hide from the "PEERS" and the rewards received from enlightened "PEERS" who realized that incentives could actually increase production much more than the cost of the incentives. Incentives were okay as long as the "COMMONS" knew their "place".

The "COMMONS" are still the creators of wealth. The freedom won in the revolution allowed the "COMMONS" to create wealth and a standard of living that was inconceivable under the authoritative English rule. For the first time in history, the "COMMONS", not the "PEERS", controlled the majority of wealth.

Since Paine's "COMMON SENSE" was written and the "LAND OF THE FREE AND THE HOME OF THE BRAVE" has won its freedom from England, a middle class has been established. The "PEERS" right to initiate force against the "COMMONS", confiscate their wealth or simply impose their will has been severely limited, but it has not been eliminated. Since Cornwallis surrendered to George Washington, the "WANNABE PEERS" have been chipping away at the "COMMONS" individual rights. The true nature of their agenda is hidden in eloquent dialogue. The "WANNABE PEERS" use promises of prosperity, redistribution of wealth, the "COMMON GOOD", demonizing an enemy and eliminating the behavior that the "BEHAVIOR CONTROL WANNABE PEERS" find objectionable to gain power. Chapter 4 will show in detail how Hitler and Mussolini used these arguments to gain power. Generally, the "WANNABE PEERS'" arguments are long on sarcasm, emotion and lies but short on logic and facts. Because of the ineffective defense of our liberty, many of the "WANNABE PEERS'" proposals have been generally accepted and are now public policy.

Poor Thomas Paine must be spinning in his grave.

The objective of this book is simply to update Paine's "COMMON SENSE" and apply its principles to the world as it exists today. A word of caution; it is possible to be a "PEER" and a "COMMON" at the same time. A "COMMON" who created considerable wealth exploiting a new technology frequently seeks government aid to suppress innovation when others develop a new technology that threatens the established industry. Attacks on individual freedom cannot be justified by one's productivity. Yes, life is not "black and white" but shades of gray. But life is gray because the good and bad are mixed. It is the individual's responsibility to separate the good from the bad and discard the bad. Life is hard.

In addition to his writing, Thomas Paine was a mechanical designer. One of his designs was a cast iron bridge conceived to replace wooden bridges that were susceptible to ice damage in the winter. His bridge concepts were never built but were seriously considered both in Europe and America. His writings clearly show the discipline and ability to redefine and simplify problems which are acquired by technical or scientific education.

The engineer uses techniques like "free body diagrams" and "systems analysis" to identify and simplify problems. These techniques also identify and isolate the irrelevant, allowing the engineer to understand and solve the problem or predict the performance of a new design. With a little imagination, many of the laws of physics have application to the evaluation of the "WANNABE PEERS" proposals. An example is

The **FIRST LAW OF THERMODYNAMICS**, the law of conservation of energy. It states that "**the energy added to a substance = the change in internal energy + the mechanical energy given out or taken in**". Paraphrased, it says that "energy can be neither created nor destroyed" or "**you can't get something for nothing**". Rigorously applied, the first law of thermodynamics debunks most of the "WANNABE PEERS" proposals.

The engineer, using "SYSTEM ANALYSIS", simplifies a problem by drawing a circle around the process and using arrows to show input and output. What occurs inside the circle is ignored.

For instance, to determine efficiency in a heat engine you divide the device's usable output by the heat input and multiply by 100 and you have the device's percent efficiency. No worries about valve timing, compression ratio, rpm or carbon dioxide emissions. You have calculated the efficiency, simply and easily by ignoring the irrelevant information. This tool, when applied to political proposals, enhances and simplifies the evaluation of those proposals.

"WANNABE PEERS" have no problem proposing violations of the laws of physics or the laws of human nature. They purposely complicate the proposals and predict unlikely, if not impossible results. The "WANNABE PEERS" won't apologize when their agenda fails to achieve the promised results. They will just accept the surrender of some of your freedom and spin another "fairy tale".

"System analysis techniques will make the evaluation and debunking of the "WANNABE

PEERS" proposals easy and help you understand their real objective.

To illustrate, let's see how these tools might have been used to avoid problems resulting from a historic disaster caused by the Government's use of force to violate an individual's rights. There are many such instances in history. One such program that occurred long ago and has been thoroughly discredited by time is "Prohibition" [1] (the Eighteenth Amendment to the Constitution).

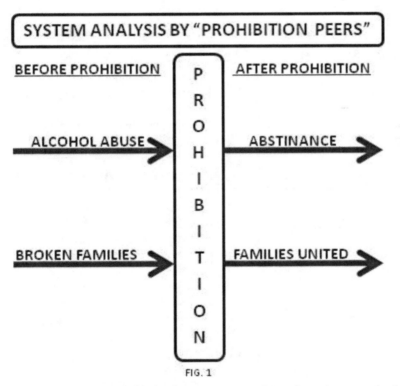

SYSTEM ANALYSIS BY "PROHIBITION PEERS"

BEFORE PROHIBITION

AFTER PROHIBITION

P R O H I B I T I O N

ALCOHOL ABUSE

ABSTINANCE

BROKEN FAMILIES

FAMILIES UNITED

FIG. 1

Prohibition resulted in violence, death and disability caused by contaminated alcohol, gun fights in the streets and political corruption, which many say continues in Chicago after over 75 years since prohibition was repealed. The measure failed to stop the use of alcohol (some say the use of alcohol increased during the prohibition years). The failure highlights the difficulty of controlling human behavior by the use of force.

The "WANNABE PEERS" used the media to saturate the country with the "preponderance of propaganda" filled with lies, sarcasm, and promises of utopia to sell the country on their scheme. The "PROHIBITION WANNABE PEERS" system analysis would have looked like Fig.1 above.

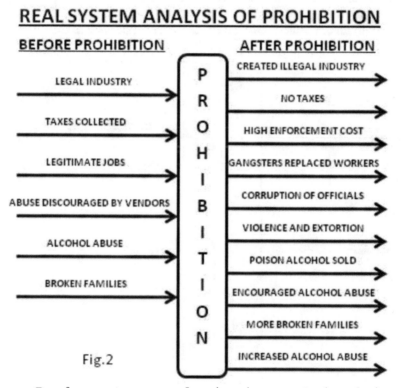

Real system analysis is contained in the chart Fig. 2, above.

With a little logic and reason, the above chart could have been created in 1918, just as easily as today, and the pain and suffering caused by that intrusion on individual freedom avoided.

Before the engineering analysis can begin, data must be collected and evaluated. The data or facts that will be used in the analysis are listed below. Many are common knowledge, but few of us understand the true implications. You may consider some controversial. Each item will be discussed, clarified in detail and proof offered at the appropriate time.

AYN RAND[3] believed that the primary purpose of the government was to protect the individual from the initiation of physical force and violence, both foreign and domestic. Freedom from the initiation of physical force and violence for all is in the long term best interest of everyone. This statement has much wider application than simply protection from robbery. For instance, the pollution which affects the life and property of others is certainly the initiation of force.

Wealth, unlike energy, can be created, destroyed and consumed. Over time, wealth (except some commodities) will become obsolete or consumed. Therefore, continuous creation of wealth is necessary to continue life as we know it and benefits the whole of society. In the late 1940's, the government had an advertising campaign with the slogan, "THE MORE WE PRODUCE, THE BETTER WE LIVE". It's as true today as it was then.

The principles and facts upon which this book is based are listed below. Historical evidence will be used to validate these principles and show how their violation has affected your life.

CHAPTER ONE

- The initiation of the use of physical force is incompatible with the creation of wealth.
- Wealth is much easier to consume or destroy than it is to create.
- Wealth must be created before it can be consumed.
- Wealth is the property of the creator of that wealth.
- Creation of wealth is defined as creating or increasing the value of an asset.
- Persecution and harassment of the "COMMONS" (producer) is not in the best interest of the consumer.
- The ingredients in the recipe for the creation of wealth are freedom, intellectual activity, labor, energy, education, capital investment, a stable government, transportation, ambition and self preservation.
- All "consumable assets" have energy content. Any increase in the cost of energy or decrease in availability of energy increases the cost and restricts the production of consumable assets.
- History has shown that the closer a society is to "pure capitalism" the more prosperous that society is.
- The capitalistic society encourages innovation. Innovation is the source of "technology dividend". (The historic growth of the "technology dividend" is discussed in Chapter2.) The book, "AN EMPIRE OF WEALTH" by John Steel Gordon[20] is also an account of how technical innovation created America's wealth. The "technology dividend" is the increase in individual

productivity that reduces the amount of effort or material required to produce wealth. An increase in the standard of living requires a corresponding increase in individual productivity.

- The "technology dividend" brings new products to market and enhances our life.
- Money is not wealth. Money is a medium of exchange. It is the creation of wealth that gives money value.
- Control of the supply of the "medium of exchange" (money) is one of the "WANNABE PEERS" most prized tools.
- Prices in a free market are controlled by supply and demand. Upon interruption or fear of an interruption of supply, the price will rise.
- Fossil fuels will be the most economical source of energy (assuming no catastrophic interference by the "WANNABE PEERS") for at least 200 years. There may be some opportunities for economical harvesting of "alternative energy" due to the terrain, constant winds, or easily available heat below the earth's crust. These situations can provide only a small fraction of the energy necessary to power our economy. However, these will be the exception, not the rule. When amortization of capital investment and intermittent availability of the energy source is considered, there is no economical substitute for fossil fuel. Nuclear power may be an exception. The "WANNABE PEERS" want the government to solve a problem that won't exist for over 200 years, yet they ignore imminent problems which offer them no opportunity to increase their power. Who will benefit

19

from this misapplication of capital? The "WANNABE PEERS" and their political cronies, of course, and most of us will surely lose.

- Carbon dioxide has not been proven to be the cause of climate change[6]. This fable has been proven only by the preponderance of the propaganda. Computer models which predict climate change based upon increased carbon dioxide do not pass back testing. Do not allow the "WANNABE PEERS" to destroy your standard of living on a quest to fight windmills that even Don Quixote would recognize. There is no issue, today, that has more potential to destroy the economy, push more of the population below the poverty line and allow the "WANNABE PEERS" to increase their control over the individual. Trying to control climate change by controlling carbon dioxide emissions would be like removing the cigarette lighter from your car to increase gas mileage.

- The "technology dividend" continuously reduces the real cost of goods and services.

- Even though the "technology dividend" continuously reduces the **real cost** of goods and services, in a real system, the cost (in currency) of goods (includes gold and other natural resources) and services **increases** due to inflation of the medium of exchange.

- Capitalism requires the continual redeployment of resources as innovation causes obsolescence of facilities and changes the demand for products. Innovation without obsolescence is impossible. This obsolescence is painful. It causes valuable labor skills and production equipment to become worthless.

- Natural resources (oil, coal, iron ore etc.) are potential wealth, just as a weight suspended in air contains potential energy and requires a machine to convert it into useful work. Natural resources require that "COMMONS" expend effort and capital to convert it into wealth.

- Innovation requires energy. Most of the "technology dividend" involves the use of energy to increase the individual's productivity. Restrict the use of energy and you reduce the individual's productivity.

- Even the most prosperous societies have finite assets. Misallocation or restrictions on the use of assets reduces prosperity. Restricting individual freedom is a restriction on the use of an asset. Political deployments of wealth (EARMARKS are an example) are usually misapplication of wealth.

- Misallocation of assets reduces prosperity and counteracts the "technology dividend".

- Increasing productivity has the greatest effect on the standard of living of the lowest level of society as it reduces the real cost of the wealth ("consumable assets") necessary for survival. Typically, the lowest level of society expends their total effort to barely survive so any reduction in the cost of survival increases the well-being of that group.

- The primary constituencies of the "WANNABE PEERS" are the lower level of society, primarily those dependent on the government aid for survival.

- The composition of their constituency is not lost on the "WANNABE PEERS". When the deception is stripped from their agenda, it becomes obvious that almost every item of their agenda will result in either destruction of wealth or restriction on the creation of wealth.

- The "WANNABE PEERS" claim the moral high ground. They claim that they are trying to help "those less fortunate", work for the "common good", provide protection from an enemy or protect us from our "vices". Yet, the "WANNABE PEERS'" every proposal limits our liberty, inhibits production and destroys or confiscates wealth.

- A favorite tactic of the "WANNABE PEERS" is to vilify a common "enemy" and use the defense against that enemy to obtain popular support. Many times the vilification is the justification for oppression and confiscation of the "enemy's" property.

- Only the individual has rights. Special rights conferred on any group must first be taken away from the individual.

- When an individual's rights are lost, the individual becomes more dependent on the government, thus giving the "WANNABE PEERS" more control over the individual's life and property. Loss of rights generally results in an increase in the "PAWN" population and a resulting increase in the "WANNABE PEERS" constituency.

- There is no government program, no matter how poorly conceived and implemented, that does not have some positive effects.
- Monopolies can exist only when backed by force.
- "BY RIGHT OF CONQUEST" before WWII this pretty much summed up the morality of foreign relations in the world. What this means is that when a nation won a war, that nation had the right to appropriate the territory and wealth of the loser. "BY RIGHT OF CONQUEST" is a principle much prized by foreign "KINGS" and their henchmen, the "PEERS". Of course, usually a nation would trump up some grievances before it attacked its neighbor. But the real cause of most wars was, and still is, the lust for the neighbor's wealth.
- As wealthy and strong as America is, it cannot feed, clothe, shelter and provide health care for the world. Subsidizing the victims of foreign "KINGS" and "PEERS" cannot provide lasting relief. As long as major portions of the world punish productivity and believe it is easier to confiscate wealth than to create it, poverty will be rampant. "KINGS" and "PEERS" can destroy and consume wealth much faster than America can create it. It is futile to try to raise the standard of living where ownership of wealth is determined by force.
- America cannot depose the "KINGS" and "PEERS" who have popular support even though they are causing widespread poverty and injustice.

- Any totalitarian government (a government totally controlled by the "PEERS" or "KINGS) requires an enemy to remain in power.
- Laws are made to prevent actions, not encourage innovation. Can you imagine Congress passing a law requiring Thomas Edison to develop the light bulb or Charles Martin Hall to develop an economical method of refining aluminum?
- The "safety net" in one form or another has existed in our society since before the year 990[12]. The question is not whether or not to have the "safety net". It seems that over 1000 years of history have settled the issue. The question is how to structure the "safety net" to provide maximum opportunity and incentive to those caught in unfortunate circumstances.

The way to evaluate political proposals is to simplify the proposal by eliminating the extraneous dialogue and charting the inputs and outputs. When the proposals are viewed in this simple form, the results are apparent.

In Thomas Paine's day, the enemy (the "PEERS" and the "KING") were identified and the solution was apparent. The solution was victory on the battlefield. Today, the identification of the "WANNABE PEERS" is difficult. The "WANNABE PEERS" carefully conceal their identity. The objective and projected results of their agenda are models of deception. Are all of these agendas that seek to limit our freedom devised with malice and forethought? Probably not; some may actually believe that some surrender of your freedom is in the public interest. They may have the purest motive or a desire to become the next "Hitler". Their motive is irrelevant. Their objective will not affect the results. Don't waste time trying to determine a politician's objectives. Evaluate the agenda. **There is no such thing as benevolent slavery**.

An understanding of the nature of government, wealth and economic systems is necessary to identify the "WANNABE PEERS" and understand their proposals. So, before the deception is stripped from their agendas a review of these subjects is provided.

CHAPTER TWO

WEALTH

Because an understanding of the nature of wealth and how wealth is created is necessary to evaluate and understand the "WANNABE PEERS" agenda, this chapter defines wealth and how changes in the nation's wealth affect society. Some important facts about wealth:

- The quantity of wealth that exists in nature is so small that the statement that wealth does not exist in nature is true. If you find wild blackberries, you have to pick them to convert the wild blackberries to "consumable assets"
- Wealth must be created from the raw materials and the opportunity that exists in nature
- Wealth cannot be consumed before it is created. It is surprising how most of the "WANNABE PEERS" agenda ignores this basic fact
- Raw material and energy require labor and intellectual activity to be converted to wealth
- An increase in the nation's wealth benefits the whole of society

There are two primary methods for the individual to accumulate wealth. The first

method is to create the wealth; the second is
to confiscate it from the creator of the
wealth. Confiscation requires force or the
threat of force causing conflict. The
conflict generally destroys a portion of
society's wealth and damages or destroys the
source of the wealth. Many times, the
conflict caused by confiscation eliminates or
reduces any advantage gained by the
perpetrator. Confiscation falls into two
categories. The first is to rob, steal or use
fraud to extract the wealth from the creator
(or the benefactor of the creator). These
methods are prohibited by laws and can lead to
sanctions against the perpetrator. The second
method is the use of government power to
provide an advantage to the perpetrator's
interest or even confiscate and transfer the
wealth. In the first case, the perpetrator is
a criminal. In the second case the
perpetrator is a "WANNABE PEER". Is there any
real difference? Of course, persecution of
the creator (producer) and confiscation of the
wealth inhibits the creation of wealth
(innovation). Much of the "WANNABE PEERS"
plan to increase their power is based upon
obtaining control of wealth and the ability to
destroy and inhibit the creation of wealth.
The destruction or inhibition of the creation
of wealth increases poverty, thus increasing
the "WANNABE PEERS" constituency.

A nation's wealth is the sum of the value
of the assets, goods and available services.
Wealth must be created before it can be
consumed and the most important ingredients in
the creation of wealth are freedom, political
stability, intelligence, and knowledge. The
creation of wealth also requires raw material

and energy. Of course, one of the functions of intelligence is to provide the raw material and energy. Unlike energy, wealth can be both created and destroyed. Wealth is consumed and most forms of wealth will eventually become obsolete and worthless due to successful innovation. This is why accounting systems have provision for amortization and depletion. Because of consumption, destruction and obsolescence, a nation's wealth is constantly being depleted; therefore, the constant replenishment of wealth is a necessity. Wealth takes many forms and may be classified as "Potential Assets", "Active Assets" and "Consumable Assets". Potential assets (Natural Resources or new technology) require the expenditure of capital to convert them into "active assets" (Reserves) before they can be used to produce "Consumable Assets". Production of "Consumable Assets" is necessary to sustain and enhance life.

POTENTIAL ASSETS:

- **Natural Resources:** natural resources are Deposits (minerals, oil, and coal) which are believed to exist. Natural resources require capital investment to prove their existence and prepare them for extraction. In the case of oil, a hole must be drilled and pumping equipment installed. As the capital investment is made, the asset becomes more valuable. Once the capital investment is successfully completed, the resources become reserves increasing the nation's wealth and providing the raw material and energy used to produce "consumable assets". If the capital investment fails to produce reserves, the capital investment is lost, reducing the nation's wealth. An excellent example would be drilling for oil and getting a "dry hole".

- **Ideas, unproven and undeveloped:** Ideas are man's greatest source of wealth. Yet, an idea unproven, undeveloped and without a market is virtually worthless. The light bulb, the telephone and the computer were once just ideas. When these ideas were developed by an entrepreneur, great wealth was produced. Natural resources, capital investment, labor and human intelligence are required to convert new ideas into wealth. Most successful inventions were once the subject of jokes and ridicule but the inventions that have succeeded in the market place were sources of great wealth. For every idea that produces great wealth, thousands flounder and the cost of those failures reduces the nation's wealth. To be successful, an idea must be sponsored by an inventor and entrepreneur (often the same person) willing to devote his fortune and total being to the success of the project. What is an idea worth? Often, the value of an idea depends on the salesmanship of its sponsor. Many ideas flounder around for years until they find an entrepreneur to champion them. How does society select an idea for development? That depends on who controls the economy. If a "KING" or "PEERS" make the decision, it is based upon political expediency and often maintaining the "STATUS QUO". A "COMMONS'" decision is based upon profit potential. Which do you think is more likely to lead to innovation and the creation of wealth?

- **Land, unused:** There are millions of acres of land in the United States that are undeveloped. Even though it is undeveloped, it has some market value and contributes to the nation's wealth. Much of this land is rich in natural resources. Tremendous wealth can be created by the development of these resources. Regulations that prevent the exploitation of these resources destroy their value and reduce the nation's wealth.

- **Human resources:** we are all "standing on the shoulders" of our forebears. Until we absorb the knowledge developed over the ages, we cannot hope to extend that knowledge. The most effective investment a government can make is the education of its citizens. At the end of World War II, the "GI BILL" was implemented to reward returning veterans for their service to the country[7]. The "GI BILL"[8] gave thousands of veterans an opportunity for a college education. Their education enhanced their productivity and led to unprecedented prosperity in post war America. The education significantly increased the ability of the veterans to produce wealth and the whole nation benefited. The wealth created by the "GI BILL" greatly exceeded the cost and the benefits of that program continue today.

- **ACTIVE ASSETS:** "Active Assets" are production facilities that have been built or developed and are producing consumable wealth. Examples of active assets are:

- **"Reserves":** Reserves are contained in oil wells and mines. The contents of these

30

reserves will be depleted and will have to be replaced. Failure to replace these reserves will result in the reduction of the nation's wealth. However, the reserves may be replaced by other forms of wealth. Technological advances can increase or reduce the demand (and thus the value) of reserves. Natural resources with the lowest capital requirements and extraction costs are depleted first. Over time, the difficulty of converting "resources" to "reserves" increases and the extraction difficulty of the reserves increase. However, the conversion and extraction costs do not necessarily increase. Fortunately, innovation tends to balance the increasing difficulty of harvesting the resources. Since the beginning of the "Industrial Revolution", technology has always increased efficiency and provided new sources of wealth to compensate for the depletion of the more easily available resources. Our nation's wealth continues to increase despite the depletion of the more easily harvested natural resources. Technology, aided by a mostly capitalistic economic system, guarantees us of an expanding economy and improved standard of living but only if we protect our system from the "WANNABE PEERS".

- **Manufacturing facilities**: Manufacturing facilities are the tool used to create the "Consumable Assets" and are defined as "active assets". The value of manufacturing facilities is not depleted like the contents of mines and oil wells, but manufacturing facilities do wear out and become obsolete. Eventually, the

31

equipment will become obsolete or wear out. The need for the product's function may be eliminated through innovation, or its products may simply go out of fashion. The manufacturing plant, once a very valuable asset, eventually will become a liability, a casualty of technological progress. To maintain and enhance the nation's wealth, the creation of new manufacturing facilities, making new products is necessary.

- **Infrastructure:** The structures and facilities required to operate our civilization. The value of the capital investment in infrastructure almost defies imagination. Infrastructure produces both goods and services required for civilization to function. Much of the infrastructure is owned and maintained by the government. The infrastructure provides facilities for transportation of goods, distribution of power, water and disposition of sewerage. When infrastructure is created, it becomes part of the country's wealth. Often a relatively small investment in the infrastructure can cause tremendous increase in the value of other assets. An example is the ERIE CANAL[2]. The ERIE CANAL opened up an entire section of the country for commerce. The increase in the value of the land served by the canal exceeded the cost of the canal by a factor of hundreds. The reduction of transportation cost added value to the products, making it economical to produce agricultural products in the area served by the canal. The ERIE CANAL was a large part of the capital investment required to convert the "Potential Asset" (unused land) into an "Active Asset". The cost of the ERIE CANAL was insignificant compared to the increase in the nation's wealth. Unfortunately, not all investments in infrastructure are as successful as the ERIE CANAL. For each "home run" like the ERIE CANAL there are many that simply consume the wealth. An example is a "WANNABE PEERS" project to invest in useless infrastructure such as the famed "bridge to nowhere" once planned for Alaska. Since the government owns and operates most of the infrastructure, many of the decisions on what and where to create infrastructure are made by "WANNABE PEERS". Of course, the "WANNABE PEERS" will make the decision based upon political expediency, not on profit potential that increases in the "Nation's Wealth". The creation and maintenance of infrastructure is vital to the economy, but it probably has more potential for the misallocation of capital than any other form of investment in our society. Since wealth is finite, wealth wasted on government boondoggles prevents the creation of worthwhile projects. Misallocation of wealth is destruction of wealth that enhances the long term objective of the "WANNABE PEERS".

- **Transportation companies, Wholesale & Retail Facilities, Builders, Service providers, Professional and other businesses which have value:** Often "consumable assets" cannot be consumed at the location where they are produced. Transporting the "consumable assets" to the location where there is demand adds value

to the "consumable asset". The ERIE CANAL
provided a low cost method of transporting
the products produced in the area it
served. Before the ERIE CANAL was built,
the cost of moving products to market from
the area the canal served was prohibitive.
The availability of low cost transportation
greatly enhanced the value of the products
and created tremendous wealth.

- **Consumable Assets:**
    The third class of wealth is
"consumable assets". As the name implies,
"consumable assets" are items whose
production has been completed and are ready
for consumption. "Consumable assets"
include the manufacturers', the
wholesalers' and the retailers' inventory,
as well as privately owned inventory.
    The "systems analysis" of the national
wealth is shown in Figure (3). The
Nation's Wealth is the total market value
of Potential Assets, Active Assets and
Consumable Assets. The market value of an
asset is the price that the asset would
sell for on the open market, not its cost
or its "book" value. The "nation's wealth"
is the basis for the value of our money.
The chart, Figure (3), summarizes the
activities that create and deplete wealth.
An understanding of this chart is necessary
to understand the real effect of the
"WANNABE PEERS" agenda. The value of the
dollar rises and falls with the total value
of the "nation's wealth" and the amount of
credit and money in circulation. Changes
in the value of the dollar may occur
rapidly or may take years to fully reflect

the changes in national wealth and the amount of credit and money in circulation.

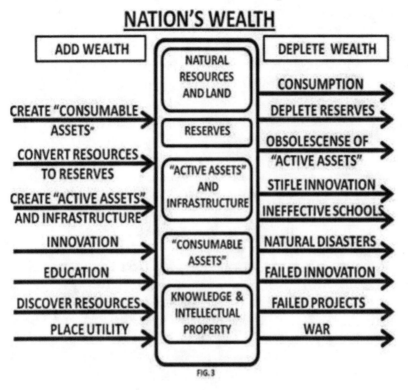

FIG. 3

Wealth and money have a confusing relationship. One of the most valuable rights afforded the individual is the right to exchange one's "best effort" for the "best effort" of others. Barter is one method of accomplishing the exchange, but barter requires two individuals who desire the other's product and that the products are of equal value. If one could simply exchange one's "best effort" for an item of recognized value that could be split into many parts and be used to exchange for many "best efforts" of others, it would simplify the transactions and facilitate commerce. Money, our medium of

35

exchange, was invented to perform this function and to store value.

Originally, money was made of precious metal and the value of the money was the intrinsic value of the metal. Paper money has no intrinsic value. What gives paper money value is the producer's willingness to accept it in payment for the producer's "best effort". It is the producer's "best effort" that gives the money value.

To facilitate the understanding of a system, often the engineer will evaluate that system at the extreme conditions. Applying that technique to the money system, consider a condition where no money or assets exist. The government decides that it wants to distribute bread to the masses and prints dollars to buy the bread. But if there is no bread, the money is worthless. If bread is produced and the producer is willing to exchange the bread for the money, the value of the money is created. At this extreme condition, the value of the dollar is the value of the bread available for purchase with the dollars. If there are no assets available or no one is willing to exchange the assets for money, the money is worthless. This condition existed in the hyper-inflation of 1920's Germany[16].

It is the value of the assets available for purchase that defined the value of money and credit in circulation. Therefore, value of the money is the value of available assets divided by the money and credit in circulation. Please see Figure (4).

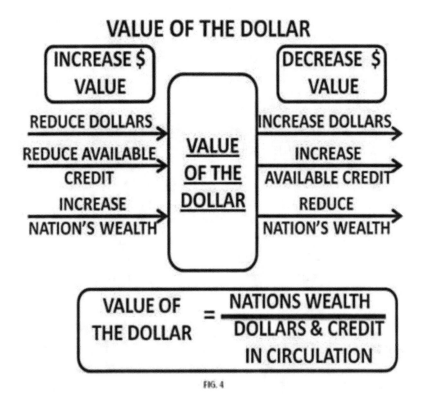

VALUE OF THE DOLLAR

INCREASE $ VALUE		DECREASE $ VALUE
REDUCE DOLLARS →		→ INCREASE DOLLARS
REDUCE AVAILABLE CREDIT →	VALUE OF THE DOLLAR	→ INCREASE AVAILABLE CREDIT
→ INCREASE NATION'S WEALTH		REDUCE NATION'S WEALTH →

$$\text{VALUE OF THE DOLLAR} = \frac{\text{NATIONS WEALTH}}{\text{DOLLARS \& CREDIT IN CIRCULATION}}$$

FIG. 4

Economic changes sometimes occur very slowly. It is possible to inflate the currency without seeing the results immediately. Technological advances reduce the material and labor content of products, constantly reducing the real cost of producing assets and increasing the amount of assets that can be produced with the available labor and material. This "technology dividend" can mask the real inflation rate.

Precious metals were used for money because its supply was limited and it could not be counterfeited. Its value was thought to be secure and inflation proof. An additional advantage was that one could carry a significant amount of wealth on one's

37

person.   However, the "KINGS" and "PEERS"
greatly prize the control of the money supply,
so ways to compromise the "inflation proof
hard currency" were quickly devised.   When
the Roman Empire started minting coins, the
"pieces of silver" were almost pure silver[22].
The pieces of silver contained considerably
less than 2 percent silver when the Roman
Empire fell.   With the acceptance of paper
money, control and manipulation of the money
supply became even easier.   Credit is a form
of money and credit is created by the banking
system.   The creation of credit increases the
apparent amount of "money" circulation. Banks
are normally allowed to lend up to ten times
the value of the sum of their capital and
deposits.   What this means is that when you
deposit one dollar in a savings account, the
bank can increase its loan portfolio by nine
dollars.   Do not despair; history shows that
economic expansion (increasing prosperity)
generally occurs in periods of slowly
expanding money supply.

Manipulation of the money supply can be
used to manage and mismanage the economy.
Generally, periods of prosperity occur when
the money supply is expanding.   Conversely, a
recession is usually accompanied by a
contraction in the money supply.   If the money
supply is increased too rapidly, the result is
hyperinflation[38].   The producer's confidence
in the money is lost and commerce is
disrupted.   The value of the individual's
money is destroyed or considerably reduced,
resulting in redistribution of real wealth.
Manipulation of the money supply gives the
"KINGS" AND "WANNABE PEERS" a powerful tool to
advance their agenda, allowing them to obtain

control of real assets just by printing money. Inflating the currency is not new. Remember the Roman Emperors, over time, significantly reduced the silver content of their coins[22]. Having to melt, dilute and strike new coins involved much more cost than just printing money. The power to control the money supply is the power to control the economy and influence the support of the "PAWNS". See Figure (4) for the Systems Analysis of the "VALUE OF THE DOLLAR". The value of the dollar change is not an instantaneous occurrence when the number of dollars in circulation changes. Time is required for the economy to detect and react to the change. The beneficial effects of the "technology dividend" mitigate the effects of increasing the money supply.

TECHNOLOGY DIVIDEND:

In a free society, the individual strives to reduce the cost and increase the value of the "best effort" that is exchanged for the goods and services produced by others. Increasing the value of this "best effort" includes both new products, reducing the cost and enhancing the performance of existing products (increasing the value). This innovation continually reduces the cost and increases the quantity of "consumable assets" created per man-hour of labor. It may also provide "consumable assets" with functions previously unavailable at any price (examples are the telephone and light bulb). The net effect of this innovation is to enhance the quality of life and/or reduce the effort the individual must expend to survive.

If the quantity of dollars and credit were to remain constant, the cost of goods and services would decline as innovation reduced the cost and enhanced the performance of consumable assets. In practice, the quantity of dollars and credit in circulation increase at a faster rate than innovation can improve productivity.

What is the rate at which the "technology dividend" accrues? One method of defining the "technology dividend" is to use the inflation adjusted per capita REAL GDP (Gross Domestic Product). Because of the availability of new products with new functions the GDP probably greatly understates the real value of the "technology dividend". The "per capita REAL GDP" (Gross Domestic Product) adjusted for inflation) has grown at a rate slightly over 2% per year during the last fifty years. Because the growth rate compounds, the actual growth rate was 184% for the last fifty years[5]. Since 1797, the inflation adjusted per capita REAL GDP grew 3,217%. The real increase in productivity is probably much greater than the GDP. It is difficult to put a value to the goods and services available today that were not available at any price in the past and the calculations for GDP in the early years is suspect.

PRODUCTION OF "CONSUMABLE ASSETS"

COST

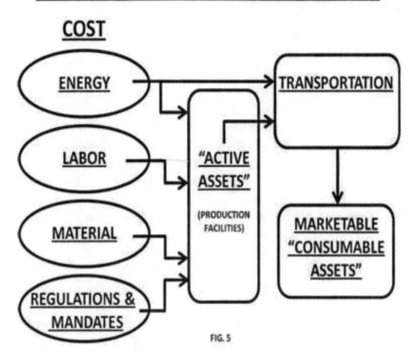

FIG. 5

Even though the use of the GDP to evaluate the "technology dividend" is flawed, it is the best available yard stick. The GDP growth understates the cumulative value of the "technology dividend" but it shows how significant the value of the "technology dividend" is to our society.

Considering the wars, government waste and the effort to maintain the "status quo" during the last fifty years, an average 2%/year is a huge increase in productivity. Without the "technology dividend" the inflation rate over the last fifty years would have been more than double the actual rate. .

VALUE OF THE DOLLAR:

CHAPTER TWO

   While the total assets of the nation
determine the value of the dollar in the long
run, the total "consumable assets" have a more
immediate effect. Figure (5) is a flow chart
showing the production of "consumable assets".
To understand the "WANNABE PEERS" agenda, one
must understand Figure 5 and its implications.
A favorite tactic of the "WANNABE PEERS" is to
vilify the producer and propose sanctions to
punish the producer. These sanctions always
increase the cost of production or reduce the
availability of the "consumable assets".
These sanctions either increase the "WANNABE
PEERS'" power or benefit a "PAWN" either as a
reward for past support or an inducement to
provide support.
   The ingredients required to produce
"consumable assets" are labor, energy,
materials, "active assets", production
facilities and transportation. The nation's
economy contains limited quantities of these
ingredients which limits the capacity to
produce "consumable assets". If there is a
change in the amount of ingredients required
to produce a "consumable asset", the value and
availability of that "consumable asset" will
change. When innovation (the "Technology
Dividend") reduces the amount of ingredients
required to produce the "consumable asset",
more of the "consumable asset" is available or
ingredients are released for other uses. The
net effect is that more "consumable assets"
become available at a **lower real cost**. All
other things being equal, the value of the
currency increases as more "consumable assets"
become available and the nation becomes more
prosperous.

If the quantity or cost of ingredients that is required to produce "consumable assets" increases, the cost of "consumable assets" increases and less "consumable assets" are available. If government regulations are implemented that require an increase in the ingredients in a "consumable asset", less of that product will be available or ingredients will be diverted from other uses. In any event, the cost of the "consumable asset" will increase. The net effect is to reduce the nation's wealth and prosperity suffers. Of course, increasing the cost of "consumable assets" has the greatest effect on the poverty stricken, the very group that the "WANNABE PEERS" profess to champion.

All "consumable assets" have energy content. Our industrial society requires tremendous amounts of energy to function. A large increase in the cost of energy will have a catastrophic effect on the economy. Proposals to combat the fairy tale that carbon emissions cause global warming will limit the availability and increase the cost of energy. Energy is one of the prime ingredients of "consumable assets" and in the transportation of those assets to market. Energy availability and cost have a tremendous effect on the nation's wealth. **Your wealth**!

Now that the relationship between wealth and money has been defined, how is wealth created?

Creation of wealth is defined as creating or increasing the value of an asset. Freedom, intellectual activity, labor, energy, education, capital investment, a stable government, transportation, ambition and self preservation are the ingredients in the recipe

43

for the creation of wealth. The cave man had
only muscles, intelligence, but minimal
knowledge and a desire to survive. His
productivity (food from uncultivated plants
and hunting small animals) required all of his
effort just to survive. But mankind's
survival depended on the mind, not physical
strength. Intelligence was used to fashion
sharp pointed sticks and clubs (innovation and
capital investment) to enhance the
productivity and provide protection from
predators.

Progress was very slow as mankind did not
treat the innovator well. Legend has it that
when Prometheus[8], a character from Greek
mythology who stole fire from the gods for
man's use, was burned at the stake for his
achievement. But mankind retained the fire.
Productivity and innovation benefit the whole
of society, but it threatens the "KINGS" or
"PEERS" power. Early mankind used the "TRIBAL
CHIEF – WITCH DOCTOR" economic system so the
"KINGS" or "PEERS" enjoyed unlimited use of
force against the producer or innovator. The
"KINGS" used this force to protect their
position of authority and confiscate most of
the wealth the "COMMONS" were able to produce.
Outstanding productivity, innovation and
attempts to protect the fruits of one's labor
were downright dangerous. There was little
incentive for the "COMMONS" to increase their
productivity as any wealth they produced
became the property of the "KING" or his
partners in crime, the "PEERS". Any
innovation that attracted attention might be
considered proof of witchcraft and result in
severe punishment or even death.

Any meaningful creation of wealth would have to wait until the producer – innovator was protected from the "KING" and "PEERS". The most important ingredient in the recipe for wealth is "freedom". For thousands of years, innovation was limited to small improvements in the agricultural industry. Wealth is created by the "COMMONS" but the "KINGS" and "PEERS" controlled the "throttle" and the "brakes" and during the "Middle Ages" the "KINGS", aided by the "PEERS", had the "emergency" brake set. The absolute power of the "KING" began to erode in the year 1215 (the Magna Carta[21]) but progress was slow. It was not until the late 18TH Century that the "COMMONS" realized that they were free to innovate and retain some of the wealth. The power of the "KING" and "PEERS" had been limited but had not been eliminated. That was the start of the "INDUSTRIAL REVOLUTION[9]". The early "INDUSTRIAL REVOLUTION" was the development of tools and processes for metal production, etc. The tools improved the efficiency of "muscle" power and the productivity of the worker, thus improving the average citizen's well being. Even with development of tools, productivity was limited by the availability of mechanical energy. Horses on a treadmill, wind and water power (where available) were the only sources to enhance the workers effort. These sources of mechanical energy were extremely limited and expensive. The only item still missing from the recipe for creation of wealth was the availability of a practical source of mechanical energy. When the "COMMONS" had freedom, knowledge and capital, it did not take them long to add the final ingredient

(ENERGY) to the recipe. Enter the "STEAM ENGINE[10]". There are descriptions of steam engines dating back to the First Century but practical use for industrial applications was not available until the early 19TH Century. The labor (man-hours) required to produce the basic necessities was significantly reduced.

Freedom, mechanical energy, tools, and education greatly improved the productivity of the "COMMONS", facilitating the creation of wealth. The productivity of the worker was greatly increased. Of course, the increase in productivity facilitated increases in consumption. But these advantages only occurred in countries where the power of the "KINGS" and "PEERS" was severely limited or eliminated. In areas where freedom was severely limited, poverty saw no relief.

The improvement in the production of machined parts is an excellent example of how the use of energy and technology enhanced individual productivity. The early lathe operator[23] applied the rotation to the spindle using a foot pedal while applying the cutting tools to the work and measuring the results. Later an apprentice on a bicycle-like device provided the rotational energy to the spindle of the lathe. The mechanical energy required to cut the metal was limited to a portion of the operator's effort or one boy power after the improvement. Cutting speed and depth of cut was severely limited because of the amount of mechanical energy that was available required considerable time to produce even the simplest product. The primary cost of the part produced was the material and labor of the two men. There was little capital investment and the energy cost little because the apprentice had to eat, anyway. Once the steam engine was available for industrial applications, a steam engine was used to power a shaft running the length of the factory. The shaft was equipped with pulleys to drive the machinery. Not only did the shaft reduce the number of people required to operate the lathe but increased the cutting speed and depth of cut that could be applied to the work. The net result was a tenfold increase in the productivity of the machinist. The addition of electric motors to the lathe increased the number of speeds and feeds available to the lathe operator further increased the operator's productivity. Then came cutting tools improvements, form tools, the automatic screw machine and the computer operated machine. The cost of metal parts was reduced and the quality was increased. This made machined parts available for uses that had been cost prohibitive before the mechanical energy became available to the machinist. Each improvement increased the productivity of the machinist. Mass produced applications requiring close tolerances became practical. The wealth of the machinist was enhanced as was the wellbeing of all who used his products. The innovation in the machine tool industry continues today. The labor content of metal parts has been reduced from "man days" to "man seconds" and less. Just think what an automobile would cost if the parts had to be machined on a lathe powered by an apprentice and each part required the attention of the operator.

All the products (agricultural, water, television, computers etc.) you use have significant energy content.

The control of available energy greatly affects the cost of everything you buy and restricting energy availability greatly inhibits the creation of wealth. Control of energy is the control of our economy and the power to destroy it, along with your job. Is it any wonder that the "WANNABE PEERS" embrace a fraudulent issue like "GLOBAL WARMING" that gives them control of energy and power to control your life? Control of energy gives the "WANNABE PEERS" a great opportunity to increase the ranks of the poverty stricken "PAWNS".

Transportation is as necessary as energy to the creation of wealth and energy cost is a large part of transportation cost. Economists have a term called "Place Utility". This means that the location of an asset affects its value. Let's look at an example to illustrate "Place Utility". You can't swim and are walking on dock. You slip and fall in the water and there is a life preserver on the dock. The life preserver could save your life, but you can't get to it. A passerby throws you the life preserver and saves your life. The life preserver had the ability to save your life but it was useless until the passerby supplied the "Place Utility". A less dramatic example of how transportation adds to the wealth of the country would be the "ERIE CANAL". The "ERIE CANAL" opened a huge area by providing an economical way to move the wealth produced in that area to market.

Wealth can be destroyed and many forms of wealth will become obsolete. As you know, it is much easier to destroy wealth than to create it. Wealth is destroyed by natural disasters, war, and failed investments.

Little can be done about natural disasters except to consider the risk when designing buildings and storing wealth. Unfortunately, nature is capable of generating conditions that exceed our specifications. When natural disasters occur, the government uses its assets to mitigate the consequences.

War is a sure destroyer of wealth and much more prolific than natural disasters. "BY RIGHT OF CONQUEST" remained the governing rule between nations, even after the "COMMONS" obtained ingredients of the recipe to produce wealth and demonstrated the advantages of creating wealth over the confiscation of wealth by use of force.

To maintain and extend their power, the "KINGS" and "PEERS" require an enemy and generally an external enemy is the most efficient choice. The principle of "BY RIGHT OF CONQUEST" and the need for an enemy to motivate the "PAWNS" are powerful incentives for the "KING" and "PEERS" belligerent behavior. The "KINGS" and "PEERS" always covet the wealth of their neighbors. For thousands of years, the principle of "BY RIGHT OF CONQUEST" was used by the "KINGS" and "PEERS" to obtain the wealth of their neighbors. It was easy to fabricate some grievance to incite the "PAWNS" to support the attack on their neighbor. The "PAWNS" could also be promised a share of the booty. The war generally destroyed the victim's ability to produce wealth. The war destroyed much wealth and the wealth seized was soon consumed. This left everyone worse off than when the adventure began but it did not stop the "KING" looking for a new victim. The instability caused by war was a major factor preventing the creation of wealth even after the Industrial Revolution began. Countries like England and Switzerland, isolated by natural barriers, fared much better than those with borders difficult to defend.

World War II is an excellent example of the invoking "BY RIGHT OF CONQUEST" principle by Russia, Japan, Italy and Germany. The need for an external enemy also was prevalent in Russia, Italy and Germany. Real and imaginary grievances were used to justify attacking their neighbor but the real reason was the lust for power and the wealth of the victim. When the principle "BY RIGHT OF CONQUEST" is invoked, misjudging your enemy's strength is disastrous and instead of obtaining wealth and power, all four countries were decimated. The infrastructure, production facilities and most consumable assets were destroyed. Russia, being on the winning side fared better, and they evoked the principle, "BY RIGHT OF CONQUEST" and confiscated the wealth and seized control of the territory of the vanquished. Russia's action caused years of poverty and misery in Eastern Europe.

The countries that won the war had considerable wealth destroyed. Even though the United States had very little infrastructure damage, five years were spent producing instruments of destruction instead of creating wealth. Instead of innovation pursuing wealth, technology was used to develop new methods of destruction.

After World War II, The United States did not invoke the principle "BY RIGHT OF CONQUEST". The United States understood the simple truth of "THE MORE WE PRODUCE, THE

BETTER WE LIVE". Everyone wins when wealth is produced rather than confiscated. The United States rebuilt its enemies. Both West Germany and Japan soon became economic powerhouses and we all benefited.

To the United States, a war is simply a danger and a drain on the economy. Unless war is necessary to maintain our freedom and way of life, it should be avoided. There is no chance of increasing the nation's wealth by use of force. Wars and threats of war (cold war) had a very negative effect on the United States economy during the Twentieth Century. Initiating the use of force destroys wealth. It does not create wealth.

The foreign "KINGS" and "PEERS" still lust for power. The need for an external enemy and wealth (which is always depleted by a totalitarian society) causes conflict with their neighbors. The supporters of the foreign "KINGS" and "PEERS" vilify the UNITED STATES because:

- The UNITED STATES provides proof to their subjects that freedom produces prosperity.
- The United States is an obstacle preventing many of the "KINGS" and "PEERS" from initiating the use of force against their neighbors.
- All "KINGS" and "PEERS" stand ready to invoke the principle of "BY RIGHT OF CONQUEST". It is not enough to create wealth. Both wealth and freedom require a constant defense.

Innovation causes obsolescence of wealth. Often the innovation is not simply an improvement in the design but a whole new technology. Once, the vacuum tube was used in

all electronic devices. When the transistor
(solid state electronics) was invented, the
vacuum tube and all the equipment used in its
manufacture became obsolete. Other fields,
not even related to electronics, like the
mechanical calculator, clocks and watches were
disrupted.   Because   of   the   required
maintenance, reliability and efficiency of the
vacuum tube, most of the devices which used
them also became obsolete and lost most of
their value very quickly. It cost less to
replace the vacuum tube equipment than to
maintain it. Even though considerable wealth
was made obsolete by the transistor, the
wealth created was far greater. Whole new
industries like the computer and "Information
Technology" became possible. The value of the
obsolete vacuum tube production equipment was
insignificant compared to the wealth created
by the invention of the transistor (solid
state electronics).

         However, if the vacuum tube production
facilities were a large part of your personal
wealth, it could have a very negative effect
on you personally. If the owners of vacuum
tube technology had successfully lobbied the
"WANNABE PEERS" to pass laws to prevent the
use of silicon, think of the effect that those
restrictions would have had on the nation's
wealth.   Innovation can have a devastating
effect on an individual, while providing great
benefits to society. Is it any wonder that
innovation always has its enemies?   It is
easy to see how the "WANNABE PEERS" can have a
devastating effect on the nation's economy,
often with only a few people even knowing
anything happened.   Remember, the "WANNABE

PEERS" are experts at hiding the real reasons and effects of their actions.

Laws seldom promote the creation of wealth. The nature of laws is to prevent actions, not encourage them. Can you imagine Congress passing a law requiring Thomas Edison to develop the light bulb? However, a law to protect the kerosene lamp industry by preventing manufacture of the light bulb is easy to imagine.

Destruction of wealth occurs when it is expended on development of worthless projects and infrastructure which has less value than its cost. Labor and material are limited resources. When labor and material are expended on worthless or losing projects, not only is the wealth expended but it is unavailable for worthy projects. Innovation requires capital. To pursue a project, the innovator must believe that the project will be profitable and either have the capital or convince investors that the project will produce a profit to obtain the capital. Of course, there is always the "charlatan" with the silver tongue to seduce the investor and skip town with the proceeds or a failure due to an honest mistake, but this method is probably the most effective at eliminating losing projects. The other extreme occurs when the "WANNABE PEERS" use the taxpayer's money on questionable projects (EARMARKS) with no thought given to the creation of wealth. The "WANNABE PEERS" only objective is to gain power or accumulate unearned wealth.

Innovation increases the nation's wealth without increasing the money supply. We will call this factor the "Technology Dividend".

The "Technology Dividend" is defined as the increase in individual productivity facilitated by the innovation.

The "Technology Dividend" is like "compound interest" as it compounds itself with each new innovation. If all other variables were held constant, the value of money would increase due to the "Technology Dividend". Without the "Technology Dividend" we would still be plowing the ground with a sharpened stick, working from dawn to dark to provide enough food to survive and maintain the "KING" in what passed for luxury before the Industrial Revolution. Productivity has been improved such that it takes a minimal amount of work to produce the necessities of life. Since the beginning of the "Industrial Revolution", even those living in poverty have been blessed with luxuries that King George III could never have imagined. Consider how indoor plumbing, the electric light, the ability to cross the Atlantic Ocean safely in a matter of hours, just to name a few of the inventions have enhanced our lives. The "Technology Dividend" has not applied equally to mankind. Where "Kings" and "PEERS" still control the government, poverty and despair are still the rule. The "Technology Dividend" is in direct conflict with the "WANNABE PEERS" objective of increasing the portion of population living in poverty. Innovation cannot be directly opposed by the "WANNABE PEERS". To oppose innovation, the "WANNABE PEERS" must use deception, for if their true objectives were to become known; they would lose their standing of moral superiority and be seen as the villains they are. Wealth is destroyed when the government imposes

54

regulations on the producer. Regulations invariably increase the material content, energy content, investment in "active assets" and/or the labor content of "consumable assets". Depending on the demand, either the price will rise or the "COMMONS" profit will be reduced. In any event, the available labor and/or material will be reduced and less of the product (or something else) will be available for consumption. The nation's wealth will be reduced. In an extreme case, the "COMMONS" could be bankrupted and the product no longer available, resulting in the loss of all the jobs in the industry (remember Prohibition). Sounds like a good way for the "WANNABE PEERS" to push more "COMMONS" below the poverty line and increase their constituency. The relationship between "COMMONS'" wealth and the "nation's wealth" is often misrepresented by the "WANNABE PEERS". The "WANNABE PEERS" often imply that there is something sinister about the "COMMONS" (producer) possessing "excessive" wealth and propose government action to limit the producer's retention and enjoyment of the fruits of his success. Figure 5 shows the relationship between the "nation's wealth" and the "COMMON'S" wealth.

Wealth (BEST EFFORT) produced by the individual "COMMON" becomes part of the "nation's wealth". In return, the "COMMON" receives money, which is exchanged for "consumable assets" (the "best effort" of others), to make investments and to pay taxes (this money goes back into circulation). In return for the taxes, governmental services and use of infrastructure are provided. If the amount of money received exceeds the consumable assets purchased, taxes and contributions, the "COMMON" will have capital available for investment. The investment might be the purchase of a home, bank deposit, stock purchase or be used to enhance the "COMMON'S" business venture. Upon investment, the money goes back into circulation. If the "COMMON" fails to invest the surplus and allows it to stagnate, the amount of money and credit in circulation is decreased, thus increasing the value of the currency. If the investment is successful, its value increases and so does the value of "nation's wealth" and the currency. The "COMMON" only has two rational choices. The wealth must be either consumed or invested. If there are no unfilled needs or desires as is the case with the most productive "COMMONS", the choice must be investment. The more ambitious "COMMONS" will forego consumption to finance pursuit of innovation. Income taxes directly reduce the capital available for investment.

One has to believe that since the "COMMON" is only concerned with the future value of the investment and the "WANNABE PEERS" are mostly concerned with reelection, that "COMMON" will choose the most efficient use of the capital. If the extra effort the "COMMONS" must exert produces only the money to pay taxes, there is little incentive for the "COMMONS" to expend that extra effort. When the marginal income tax rate was increased in the first Clinton Administration, total tax receipts actually fell. A progressive income tax reduces the availability of capital both by taxes paid and reducing the incentive of the "COMMONS" to produce wealth. A tax on productivity should be prohibited by the cruel and unusual punishment clause of the Constitution. A tax on consumption makes a lot more sense.

Innovation depends on the new ideas, effort and dedication of the "COMMONS" and is financed by the "COMMON'S" ability to produce or obtain capital. Innovation reduces the labor (increases the productivity of the individual) and/or the material content of "consumable assets". Innovation creates new products with functions previously unavailable or too costly to market. Freedom of the "COMMONS" is the most important ingredient in the recipe for the creation of wealth.

THE NATION'S AND THE "COMMON'S" WEALTH

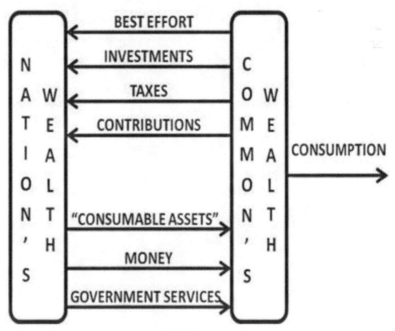

FIG. 6

The "WANNABE PEERS" will continue to try to destroy or inhibit the production of wealth in their pursuit of power and this means stifling of innovation and preventing the development of natural resources. If the "nation's wealth" and our standard of living is to continue to increase, the freedom of the "COMMONS" and their access to capital must be protected. It is the productivity (product/man-hour) of the "COMMONS" that defines the nation's wealth" and limits the consumption of wealth.

SUMMARY

Innovation, discovery and development of natural resources or invoking the principle of "by right of conquest" are the only ways to increase the nation's wealth. The use of "by right of conquest" (force) is a prescription for disaster so the only rational methods of increasing the nation's wealth are innovation, discovery and development of natural resources.

CHAPTER THREE

THE ECONOMIC SYSTEMS

"Wikipedia Encyclopedia" lists 52 different economic systems. Actually, there are only three different classes of economic systems. These are the "TOTALITARIAN", the "MIXED ECONOMY" and "CAPITALISM". Of the three classes, only "TOTALITARIAN" and "CAPITALISM" can be rigorously defined.

A "MIXED ECONOMY" is as the name implies simply a mixture of the two extremes. The balance of the "MIXED ECONOMY" constantly changes as the "WANNABE PEERS" and the "COMMONS" jockey for advantage. The long term advantage seems to lie with the "WANNABE PEERS" as it appears that our freedom erodes with time. The "WANNABE PEERS" continually attack our freedom on many fronts. They will be patient for years, knowing that once they obtain a goal, it is seldom reversed. Our near "capitalist" system is slowly being transformed into a "totalitarian" economic system.

THE "TOTALITARIAN" SYSTEM:

The "Totalitarian" system is the oldest, most disastrous and oppressive of the economic systems and is marked by instability. A simple example of the "Totalitarian" system is the Tribal Chief - Witch Doctor system, the system that has held most of Africa in abject poverty for thousands of years. The Tribal Chief seizes the wealth created by the "COMMONS". The WITCH DOCTOR then assures the "COMMONS" that they were privileged to sacrifice to the glory of the Tribal Chief and they will be rewarded for their sacrifice in the "after life". The primary characteristic of the "Totalitarian" system is the use of unlimited physical force by a "KING" (sometimes a small committee) to oppress the "COMMONS". If the political unit becomes too large to be controlled by a single individual, the "KING" empowers "PEERS" to extend his control. When possible, any achievement by the "COMMONS" is claimed by the "KING" or "PEERS". Any achievement which cannot be claimed by the ""KING" or "PEERS" diminishes their power and prestige. The fear of losing their power and prestige causes the oppression of the "COMMONS" by the "KING" and his "PEERS" and prevents the "COMMONS" from obtaining any meaningful benefit from innovation or their labor. The oppression causes discontent among the "COMMONS". Measures taken to control the discontent escalates and leads to imprisoning the dissenters and even murder by the "KING" or his henchmen, the "PEERS".   To maintain control of the "COMMONS", the "KING" invents an enemy. The "COMMONS" are taught to hate or fear this enemy more than the "KING".   An enemy is necessary for the survival of the "totalitarian" government". Once the fear of the enemy is established, dissenters can be suppressed by accusing them of collaboration with or giving support to the enemy. This deception disguises the suppression, preventing the other "COMMONS" from recognizing the injustice. Generally, the enemy is external, but occasionally an internal enemy is selected. This usually occurs when the "WANNABE KING" is trying to obtain power. Hitler's selection of the Jews as an enemy while trying to obtain power is an example. The "totalitarian" form of government prevented innovation and progress for thousands of years, but when a "KING" achieves control of an industrial society, it can function for years before the economy collapses. Declining productivity caused by economic decisions based upon political expedience and oppression of the "COMMONS" causes increased dissent. The dissent threatens the "KING'S" power and further weakens the economy. The thirst for more power and declining ability of the economy to create wealth cause the "KING'S" relations with the "necessary enemy" to become more aggressive. Eventually, either the conditions become so bad that a revolution replaces the "KING" or the "KING'S" attempts to extract wealth from the "necessary enemy" causes a war. If the war is won, the distribution of some of the confiscated wealth and patriotic fervor gives the "KING" wide popularity and allows for the consolidation of power, extending his reign. Losing the war generally results in the "KING'S" power being destroyed and the "COMMONS" losing whatever wealth they had been able to hide from the "KING". Without the intervention of a benevolent outside force, the fall of the "KING" will simply result in a new "KING" seizing power. Either way, the cycle starts over. The aggressive behavior of "Totalitarian" governments is the main source of the world's political instability. The fear of attack by a foreign "KING" causes free countries to expend considerable wealth for protection.

Do not be fooled, the "Totalitarian" system goes by many names such as Fascism, Socialism, Communism, Kingdom and some that use religious doctrine to justify the blatant use of force against the "COMMONS" and their neighbors. Call them what you will, there is no real difference. All are characterized by total power exercised by an individual or small group and oppression of the "COMMONS".

Relatively free countries look with horror at the conditions that exist in the "Totalitarian Societies" and frequently try to reduce the suffering of the "COMMONS" in those countries by supplying necessities. Trying to intervene in the plight of the "COMMONS" while the "Totalitarian" control is maintained is futile; aid simply strengthens the "KING" and prolongs the "COMMONS" plight.

"CAPITALISM"

The opposite extreme of a "Totalitarian" system is "CAPITALISM". Capitalism is an ideal that has never actually existed; it is analogous to "absolute zero" in thermodynamics. Capitalism is simply an economic system based upon maximum individual freedom. If the economic system is based on individual freedom, the government would be limited to protecting the individual from the initiation of force, both foreign and domestic. Because the term "capitalism" is not well understood, the "WANNABE PEERS'" agenda will be evaluated by the effect on individual freedom. Pure "CAPITALISM" may not be practical and might even evolve into a

"Totalitarian" system. However, history indicates that the freer a society is, the more prosperous it is. (This is analogous to a heat engine which becomes more efficient as the temperature of its heat sink approaches Absolute Zero.) When The United States won its freedom, the system established was as close to maximum individual freedom (capitalism) as has ever existed. The "WANNABE PEERS" have taken a toll on our freedom and moved our economic system ever closer to the unthinkable extreme, a totalitarian system.

In a free ("Pure Capitalist") society, the government's power would be very limited. Military force to provide protection from foreign "KINGS" would certainly be a necessity. A domestic police force would be required to maintain domestic tranquility and protect both the individual and public property from the initiation of force. Government owned or controlled infrastructure would be required to allow the police and army access to provide this protection. A court system would be required to enforce contracts, maintain a record of property ownership, settle disputes and correct injustices when one citizen initiated the use of force against another citizen. Fraud, of course, is a form of force as is any action contaminating private or common property such as the atmosphere, public lakes and streams. The government would be responsible for the management of public property. Unclaimed lands, streams, lakes, beaches, infrastructure required for civil and National Defense are examples of this property.

Taxes would have to be levied to pay for these services and taxes are an infringement on freedom (but not a grievous infringement if levied equally and used to pay for services, **not to control behavior**}. Wherever possible, taxes should be linked to the services provided. In a free society, many of the government services could be paid for with the "Technology Dividend" by inflating currency at the rate that productivity improves. Properties owned by the government would be maintained or disposed of for the equal benefit of all citizens.

There are some other less obvious government activities that could be justified because they enhance the general welfare and support the government's obligation to provide for the common defense and maintain domestic tranquility. A very strict interpretation of capitalistic principles might rule out government involvement in such activities programs as education or the "safety net". Such an interpretation would ignore some important facts. For instance, one could argue that government involvement in education is required in a Capitalistic society because an educated citizen is required for the nation's defense in a highly technological world. Education is one example of government responsibility that is not obvious from the strict definition of individual freedom ("Pure Capitalism"). Encouragement of the individual's education does not mean that the government should operate the school system.

The so called "safety net"[12] for the "unfortunate" might also be justified by the government's responsibility to protect the individual from crime. An individual without food or shelter is in a desperate situation. Without an alternative, the individual will probably resort to violence to survive. Even if you have no compassion for the "unfortunate", a case could be made that it is more economical (and humane) to provide minimum subsistence and aid for rehabilitation to the unfortunate than deal with the crime that such desperation causes.

A philosophical justification of the "safety net" appears to be irrelevant. In our society, forms of the "safety net"[12] were in existence as early as the Tenth Century; our citizens just don't want to see people dying from malnutrition and exposure in the streets. So it looks like the "safety net" will be with us. The best policy is to structure it to offer the maximum opportunity and incentive for those caught in unfortunate circumstances to rejoin the productive society.

Some may consider the reasoning that justifies the "safety net" and "public education" in a free society somewhat of a reach. At worst these initiatives (properly implemented) would have little effect on freedom and could greatly enhance the general welfare. The initiatives of education and the "safety net" may well be necessary to maintain our freedom, but the current implementation of these initiatives certainly fails to do the job.

MIXED ECONOMY:

In 21ST Century America, we live in a "mixed society". A good definition of the "mixed society" is the graph shown in Figure (7). The graph is a plot of prosperity vs. freedom. The "totalitarian society" is shown zero and the "capitalism" is at the maximum extreme on the freedom scale. A "mixed society" is any space between these two extremes.

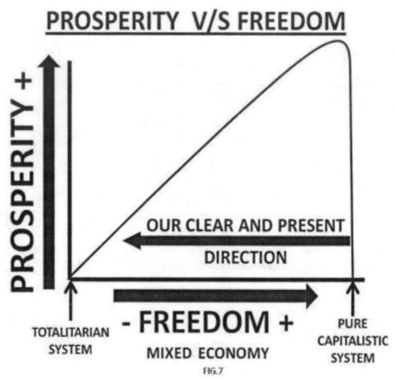

PROSPERITY V/S FREEDOM

PROSPERITY +

OUR CLEAR AND PRESENT DIRECTION

TOTALITARIAN SYSTEM

- FREEDOM +

MIXED ECONOMY

PURE CAPITALISTIC SYSTEM

FIG.7

Historical evidence indicates prosperity increases with freedom. Claiming to support the general welfare, the government of a "mixed society" will use the "WANNABE PEERS" version of "benevolent coercion" (the use of force, real or implied) to control reluctant individuals. This action differentiates it from the "capitalistic" ideal. Seldom does the use of force against an individual accomplish long term desirable results. Education and logical persuasion are much more effective in creating real and lasting change. "Benevolent coercion" rarely produces desirable long term results and should be avoided except in emergencies (danger from foreign powers).

Both the shape and values shown in Figure 7 are subjective and based upon the author's understanding of history. The graph shows prosperity reaching a maximum somewhere between the "Capitalism" and "Totalitarian" system, but much closer to the "Pure Capitalism". History actually shows only that prosperity increases with individual freedom.

There is no historical evidence available for the area of the graph where the "mixed economy" approaches "pure capitalism. There is no evidence because "pure capitalism" has never existed. The old saying "power corrupts and absolute power corrupts absolutely"[13] applies to all humanity. Without any restraints, a totally unfettered and very successful individual could use economic power to facilitate a coup, thus obtaining the power of a "KING" and creating a "Totalitarian" system. Of course, once an individual obtained the ability to initiate physical force, it would no longer be a capitalist system. Someday, society may need safeguards to prevent this type of coup. The danger of losing our freedom through the attrition of the "WANNABE PEERS" agenda is much greater than that of a coup by an industrial giant. The task of providing safeguards to prevent such a coup can safely be delegated to future generations. Today, our society is much closer to the "totalitarian" side of the graph than the "capitalist" side. Failure to act soon to reverse the trend will result in America's first "retro generation" and it may become impossible to recover our individual freedom.

CHAPTER THREE

Is prosperity desirable? A stupid question, you say. Not so. Listen to the "WANNABE PEERS" touting "global warming"[7]. True to the principles of the "preponderance of propaganda", they only promise that their program will end human induced climate change. They don't talk about the consequences of their program or that there is no proof that climate change is caused by human activity. The Don Quixote of literature attacked the windmills, believing them to be enemies of mankind. The modern Don Quixote (the "WANNABE PEERS") would have us build windmills and engage in other forms of "energy alchemy". Make no mistake about it the "WANNABE PEERS'" "energy alchemy" will only increase the cost of your energy. All "consumable assets" contain energy. When available energy is reduced or the cost of energy increases, the capacity to produce "consumable assets" is decreased and the cost of consumable assets that are produced increases. Advocating reduced energy availability and increased energy cost is advocating a reduction in prosperity, by definition. The "WANNABE PEERS" are not stupid. They have to recognize the consequences of their proposal, though many of their supporters may actually believe the propaganda. The advocates of the human induced "global warming" theory are telling us that even continuing energy use at the current levels is "environmental suicide". The truth is that the "WANNABE PEERS'" "energy alchemy" will end your life as you know it and will have no effect on the climate.

Is prosperity desirable? Certainly, but there are those among us who disagree and would destroy our freedom and prosperity based upon a theory that has been proven only by the dire predictions of disaster if the theory is valid. Why would anyone advocate such drastic actions without some proof of validity of the theory? Remember, prosperity is not in the best interest of the "WANNABE PEERS". The "WANNABE PEERS" find it much more difficult to expand their power during periods of prosperity. The "WANNABE PEERS" know that prosperity erodes their constituency.

Our priority should be to determine which of the issues that have limited our freedom (many with more negative than positive results) should be rescinded or modified. Remember, all programs have produced some positive results for some group or individual. Don't dwell on the positive results without evaluating the consequences. The "WANNABE PEERS" will only tell about the positive results.

Any proposal that violates the principles of individual freedom involves the use of force against the "COMMONS". These proposals range from taxation structured to control behavior, to confiscation of property, to incarceration for victimless crimes and sanctions for violation of non-objective laws or unclear regulations that have the force of law. An example is the "income tax code" which has been expanded beyond the capability of any individual to understand and comply with it. When you file your income tax return you can never be sure that there is no error that could result in sanctions.

Does the proposal violate our freedom? The test is simple. In a free society, the citizen would be free to engage in any activity that did not infringe on the rights

69

of others.   Does the proposal violate that
right?   To evaluate a proposal that violates
the principles of individual freedom, it is
important to determine if the loss of freedom
is worth the promised benefit and if the
promised benefit is valid.   One should also
consider the difficulty in regaining the
freedom if the promised benefits do not
accrue.   Rarely is the loss of the "COMMON'S"
freedom in the best interest of anyone.

Many of the current government activities
conflict with individual freedom.   Some may
enhance the lives of some group but all
threaten our liberty. To maximize individual
liberty, laws would be simplified and many
repealed. There would be no victimless crimes.
This means that laws regulating individual
behavior, such as those controlling drug and
prostitution, would be limited to regulations
that protected the public safety and ensuring
that erratic behavior caused by drugs took
place only in a controlled environment.
Sanctions imposed on the perpetrators of
crimes would involve restitution instead of
incarceration except when required to control
violence. The force of the government would be
used to ensure restitution and control the
behavior of the criminal (including continuous
tracking the perpetrator's location using GPS
technology) until the restitution was
completed and the perpetrator's tendency
toward antisocial behavior was corrected.
Incarceration would be used only in cases
where the public safety is an issue or close
supervision is required to force the
perpetrator to make restitution.   The
technology exists to monitor the location of a
subject and this technology should be used to

limit incarceration of offenders to those who pose a threat of violence.

The preceding paragraphs are not meant to be an exhaustive definition of a "mixed society". The purpose is to give the reader an understanding of our economic system and the principles that can be used to improve it. Perhaps absolute individual freedom is not a practical economic system, or at least it may be unacceptable to a majority of the citizens. There is no point in a more lengthy and rigorous definition of capitalism.

In a "MIXED ECONOMY" with a high degree of individual freedom, innovation would cause continual change as old processes and products become obsolete and are replaced by new and more efficient systems. Even though these innovations cause increased wellbeing in the general population, they will cause despair among those who find old skills obsolete or who own the facilities made obsolete by the innovation. Unfortunately, individual economic reverses caused by innovation may change prosperous "COMMONS" to "PAWNS" or "WANNABE PEERS", who try to use the force of the government to protect the "status quo". The argument they use will not condemn progress but will use some fabricated reason, such as environmental damage, loss of jobs or even religious dogma. These deceptive arguments can be very effective especially when no campaign opposes the argument. Accepting those deceptive arguments will stifle the compounding of the "Technology Dividend".

Innovation can be very painful in the short run, to those who stand to lose their livelihood or see their property values

71

diminish as a result of innovation. When the government uses its monopoly on force to prevent innovation, we all lose in the long run. Part of the "Technology Dividend" could be used to mitigate the individual losses caused by innovation. Any programs implemented to reduce the impact of innovation should be to aid the victims to recover their productivity, not maintain the "status quo". Any assets expended to mitigate the pain of change will reduce the assets available for supporting innovation and the growth of the "technology dividend" will be adversely affected.

There are government actions which violate the strict principles of individual freedom that enhance the general welfare with loss of little individual freedom. The "Erie Canal" is an example. Public funds provided by taxation were used to build the canal for purely economic reasons. The canal provided an economic bonanza for the entire region and greatly enhanced the general welfare with very little encroachment on individual freedom. The "Erie Canal" may be one of the best arguments in favor of a "Mixed Society". The Erie Canal is definitely one of the few government projects that achieved increased general prosperity without oppression of some group of citizens. Any proposed government project that violates the principles of individual freedom should be carefully evaluated before it is implemented. Proponents of this type of project should first use education and persuasion to find private capital for financing. Failure to be able to obtain private capital is a powerful argument against any project but there are projects (like the Erie Canal) that can enhance the general welfare but do not have the profit potential required for private investment.

The Erie Canal is the exception, not the rule. Most government initiatives that violate the principles of individual freedom have negative if not disastrous results. Examples are Prohibition, imprisonment of American citizens of Japanese descent during World War II, attempts to limit inflation by the use of price controls and of course slavery, just to name a few.

Prosperity is a major consideration in the choice of the balance of our "Mixed Economy" but we must not forget that enhancing the general welfare is also important. Though, prosperity and the general welfare seem to complement each other.

The balance of the "Mixed Economy" that yields maximum prosperity and general welfare will have to be found by trial and error. It is quite likely that some minor violations of individual freedom could result in enhancing the general welfare. The enactment of safeguards to avoid an economic coup (as described above) is certainly an example. Currently, we are well below "peak prosperity" and much closer to the "Totalitarian" economy. Many of the government programs that were enacted to apply "benevolent coercion" have been shown to be somewhat lacking in the "benevolent" department and many should be rescinded or modified to allow them to reach their original objective. Of course, to accomplish this we will need politicians more interested in increasing prosperity than increasing the "WANNABE PEER'S" constituency.

CHAPTER THREE

Any law or program that prohibits an action by an individual, where the action does not infringe on the rights of others is a violation of individual freedom. There are many "WANNABE PEERS" programs which fall under this definition. All these programs should be examined and most, if not all, should be eliminated. The general welfare is rarely served by restricting individual freedom. Some of these programs may yield positive results (but often temporary) and for a minority at the expense of society as a whole. These programs will be vigorously defended by those who believe they are benefiting.

The philosophical defense (by Ayn Rand) of maximum individual freedom ("Pure Capitalism") is that it is in everyone's "long term rational selfish best interest" that everyone is protected from the "initiation of physical force". This, of course, is a one sentence oversimplification of Ayn Rand's philosophy[3], by an engineer, not a philosopher. Ayn Rand[3] believed that the initiation of force against an individual is immoral. The website www.**aynrand.org** or her books, "THE FOUNTAINHEAD" and "ATLAS SHRUGGED" will provide the reader with more information on Ayn Rand's philosophy and writings.

The "Mixed Society" is a mixture of freedom and benevolent coercion by the government. America was never a "Pure Capitalistic" society and some of the coercion was not very benevolent. The Post Office was certainly not a capitalistic enterprise; however, The Founding Fathers felt the Post Office was necessary to ensure communications. Slavery was certainly an exception, as was the treatment of the "Tories" (British sympathizers) after independence was won. The principle of "by right of conquest" was applied to the original inhabitants of America. The initiation of physical force against the Indians was certainly a violation of individual freedom. In the late Eighteenth and early Nineteenth Centuries, "by right of conquest" was still a generally accepted principle and the "Technology Dividend" had not had significant time to accrue. Survival was still a very difficult proposition and many man-hours were required to produce the "Consumable Assets" required to survive. Many contradictions to individual freedom and even human behavior as we understand it today existed in the early United States. We cannot judge the "COMMONS" too harshly for flexing their muscle. Remember, the "COMMONS" were emerging from thousands of years of oppression during which the guiding principle was "by right of conquest" and the only way to obtain wealth was the use of force. Is it any wonder that the Colonies were less than hospitable to those perceived to be outsiders?

Before the United States won its independence, there was no such thing as a free society and there was much disagreement as to what a government should be. George Washington is reported to have turned down efforts to declare him "KING"[18] several times. Even though no "blueprint" for a free society existed, the "Founding Fathers" were able to establish a society with most individuals free to create and enjoy the wealth they created. The "Technology Dividend" exploded. The "Founding Fathers" created a "Mixed Society" that produced unprecedented wealth, even

CHAPTER THREE

though that society was a mixture of freedom,
benevolent coercion and sometimes initiation
of force against the individual. The
formation of the government did not resolve
the question of what the government should be.
It just started the "trial and error" effort
to create a better government. The
"COMMONS", concerned with innovation and
creation of wealth, competed with the "WANNABE
PEERS", whose objective was personal power.
The "WANNABE PEERS", using deception and
patience, have been successful in having much
of their agenda enacted into law. The
benevolent coercion has become less benevolent
and the loss of freedom more onerous with
time. The increase in the "benevolent
coercion" part of the equation has been mixed,
occasionally promoting prosperity. Most often
"benevolent coercion" has been a pressure
group seeking advantage over fellow citizens.
Surrender of liberty seldom provides any
lasting good. Benevolent coercion is rarely in
the long term best interest of either the
coerced or the beneficiary. If it were, would
coercion be required? If it is truly in the
citizen's best interest, would it not be
better to gain compliance through education
and logical persuasion than the use of force?
Of course, issues like funding the "common
defense" require participation of all
citizens. All citizens reap the benefits of
economic and political stability provided by
the "common defense".

If there were any doubt as to which
economic system produced the better standard
of living, it should have been resolved by a
tale of two Koreas.

In the early 1950's, the Korean War left the Korean peninsula decimated. At the end of the war, the "Totalitarian" government of North Korea remained in power in contrast to South Korea's mixed economy (mostly capitalistic government). Since that time, South Korea's economy[4] has grown to be rated fourth in Asia and thirteenth in the world. North Korea's economy[4] is now twenty-eight in Asia and eighty-fifth in the world. South Korea's "GDP" (gross domestic product) is almost 37 times the North Korean GDP. Even these figures do not adequately describe the famine and misery existing in North Korea.

All the historic evidence shows that the system which provides the most individual freedom provides its citizens with the highest standard of living and more satisfying life. Yet, the United States continues to adopt the portions of the "WANNABE PEERS'" agenda which limit freedom, even though most of the country's problems can be traced to the loss of freedom and restrictions placed on the economy by that agenda. This divergence from "Capitalism" seems to be accelerating. If this trend is not reversed, it will be difficult to recover our freedom. The success of the "WANNABE PEERS" agenda continually increases the ranks of those dependent on the government, enlarging the "WANNABE PEERS" constituency and making recovery from the trend toward the "Totalitarian" society more difficult to reverse.

The government controls vast wealth. Consider the infrastructure, public lands, military hardware, military bases, the postal system, the public school system, airports, the National Parks, government buildings, the

77

gold stored in Fort Knox and other wealth too numerous to mention. The government is similar to a corporation where each citizen is a stockholder. It is the government's responsibility that each citizen benefits equally from the government's wealth. The "Technology Dividend" has had over two hundred years to compound and the man-hours required to produce the "Consumable Assets" required for survival has been reduced to very low levels. Options available for providing aid to the unfortunate are now available at minimal cost to society. Justification for this aid is presented by the vast wealth controlled by the government and the "Technology Dividend" which are the property of every citizen, even though such aid might conflict with some people's concept of "Pure Capitalism". Properly configured, such aid could enhance the productivity of many of the unfortunate and increase prosperity and the general welfare.

RECIPE FOR EVALUATION OF PROPOSALS:

The "WANNABE PEERS" are constantly proposing new assaults on our freedom and wealth. These proposals are always preceded by a "preponderance of the propaganda" that extols the virtue of the proposal and total neglect of any adverse affects. The principles that assure individual freedom and creation of wealth have been used to develop a list of questions to help the reader evaluate these proposals. A "yes" answer to any question should raise serious questions about the proposal. The proposal should be rejected, outright, or given serious and detailed analysis.

QUESTION: Does the proposal favor a special group?

PRINCIPLE: Every citizen is equal under the law. Special "rights" awarded to any group diminishes the freedom of all.

QUESTION: Is the purpose of a proposed tax to control behavior?

PRINCIPLE: The legitimate purpose of taxes is to raise revenue. A tax to control behavior is a violation of individual freedom, usually proposed after a campaign to vilify the behavior. The real reason of the "WANNABE PEERS" is usually the desire to raise taxes and increase the amount of wealth controlled by the government, while obtaining support from those who would use government force to control individual behavior.

QUESTION: Does the proposal increase the cost of producing "consumable assets"?

PRINCIPLE: Campaigns to vilify the producer often precede the proposal for government controls on production or performance of a product. Government controls always raise costs which are passed on to the consumer or reduce availability of the "consumable asset". Punishing the producer is not in the best interest of the consumer.

QUESTION: Does the proposal make it more difficult or illegal to harvest natural resources?

PRINCIPLE: Inability to harvest natural resources inhibits the creation of wealth. Current restrictions have impacted our standard of living, increased government control of our individual behavior and had a disastrous effect on our foreign policy.

QUESTION: Does the proposal limit the use of private property?

PRINCIPLE: Limiting the use of private property reduces the value of that property and is actually a tax applied against the owner of the property. It is grossly unfair to use legislation to seize the use of private property without just compensation to the owner. It diminishes the freedom of all. This includes zoning laws, land use laws and environmental restrictions enacted to benefit a mutant fish in a temporary mud puddle.

QUESTION: Does the proposal seek to protect the "status quo" at the expense of innovation and progress?

PRINCIPLE: Growth of prosperity (innovation) requires continuous redeployment of resources to develop new products and processes. Innovation obsoletes both assets and labor skills, causing economic losses to those adversely affected. Displaced industry and labor often try to mitigate their losses by using government force to stifle progress.

QUESTION: Will the proposed project consume more wealth than it produces?

PRINCIPLE: Many proposed government projects are selected based upon political expedience rather than economic worth. This is especially true of projects that have commercial applications. Projects that will produce good profits have no problem raising capital to develop them. Charlatans frequently try to obtain government funding for questionable projects that private capital shuns.

QUESTION: Will the proposal diminish your freedom?

PRINCIPLE: Enough said.

SUMMARY:

In succeeding chapters many of the current specific government programs are evaluated. To highlight the effects of the use of government force against the individual, several historical programs will be studied in depth and the disastrous results exposed. Recommendations will be made based upon the analysis. All recommendations will enhance individual freedom and prosperity. Of course, enhancing the "COMMON'S" freedom and prosperity will destroy some of the power of the "WANNABE PEERS" and deplete their constituency as prosperity reduces the ranks of the poverty stricken.

CHAPTER FOUR

"KINGS" and "WANNABE PEERS" – TWENTIETH CENTURY DICTATORS

"Those who cannot remember the past are condemned to repeat it".[14] GEORGE SANTAYANA, philosopher.

Recent history provides many examples of a mixed economy degenerating into a totalitarian dictatorship. We should be familiar with the personal characteristics, tactics and conditions that allowed these dictators (Mr. Paine's "KINGS") to achieve "absolute power" completing the degeneration of a mixed economy into a totalitarian dictatorship.

Lest we forget; we should study how these Twentieth Century dictators achieved total destruction of individual freedom and brought chaos to their countries and the entire world. The Twenty-First Century "WANNABE PEERS" ambition may not be to become a dictator. Their intentions are irrelevant. Each success of the "WANNABE PEERS" will just whet their appetite for more power, until our freedom is totally destroyed and chaos reigns. If our freedom is usurped, there will be no United States to save the world!

"**Power tends to corrupt, and absolute power corrupts absolutely.**" – A quote[13] from a letter by John Emerich Edward Dalberg-Acton, 1st Baron Acton, written in April 1887. The quote is as true today as it was in 1887 and it has been validated by history. If there were any doubt, the 20TH Century provided many examples that demonstrated the validity of the quote. Three of the dictators who obtained absolute power were **Benito Amilcare Andrea Mussolini**[15], **Adolf Hitler**[16], and **Fidel Alejandro Castro Ruz**[17].

Both Hitler and Mussolini converted a mixed economy (an ailing mixed economy) into a dictatorship. The factors the "WANNABE PEERS" used to their tactical advantages were:

- Economic crisis
- Exploitation of the "preponderance of propaganda"
- Financial support from wealthy patrons seeking to use the governments' monopoly on force for personal benefit or perhaps just protection from other "WANNABE PEERS'" or thugs
- Physical intimidation, the initiation of force against their political opponents, taking advantage of the failure of the government to protect individuals or groups from the initiation of physical force. Protection from initiation of physical force is the most basic function of the government and some would say the only reason for the existence of government. (Did you ever wonder why the "WANNABE PEERS" advocate gun control? Initiation of force against an armed individual is a

risky affair and the results cause adverse publicity and civil unrest.)

- Compromise, the trading of special favors for power. (Used very effectively by Hitler to crush the opposition and give him total control of the government once he became Chancellor)
- Alliance against a common enemy
- Charismatic personality
- Extraordinary communication skills
- The fallacy that there is a real difference between the three forms of Totalitarianism (Communism, Fascism and Socialism)

All nine of these factors were necessary for the "WANNABE PEERS" to obtain and consolidate their power. Both Hitler and Mussolini benefited from the popular fallacy that:

Fascism is on the extreme right of the political spectrum with both Communism and Socialism on the extreme left.

The truth is that all three are just Totalitarian governments on the extreme left and individual freedom (capitalism) on the right.

Castro used revolutionary force to displace another dictator, Fulgencio Batista y Zaldivar. The Castro Regime is more of interest to show how difficult it is to regain freedom through a revolution and how a repressive dictator can maintain power, while the country wallows in poverty and oppression of individual liberty. Look back at early American history to see how easily George Washington[18] could have been an Eighteenth

84

Century Castro. History shows how rare George Washington was and how fortunate the world was to have him lead the American Revolution.

Was the original goal of these tyrants to become a dictator? Who knows? Who cares? Their original intentions are irrelevant; the results of their actions are all that are important. While pursuing power they preached patriotism, prosperity and protection from a common enemy; what they provided was a Totalitarian government with misery, poverty and destruction.

BENITO AMILCARE ANDREA MUSSOLINI[15]

The Italian Fascist's coup preceded Hitler's regime by ten years and seems to have few, if any advocates today, so it is less controversial than the NAZIS. Being less controversial, it is much easier to be objective so we will study Mussolini's coup first. Mussolini's rise to power is a classic case study in the destruction of individual freedom and creation of a Totalitarian Society.

Mussolini was born to working class parents July 29, 1883. His mother was a school teacher and his father was a blacksmith. The father was a Socialist with a distain for authority which he passed on to his son, along with his Socialist leanings. Mussolini was an unruly child, once expelled (at age 11) from a boarding school for stabbing a student in the hand and throwing an inkpot at a teacher. However, he was a good student when his violence was controlled. He eventually achieved elementary schoolmaster status in 1901. His Socialist leanings caused him to immigrate to Switzerland in 1901 to escape military service. He was deported from

CHAPTER FOUR

Switzerland after joining the Socialist Movement but soon returned and the Swiss Socialist found him a job in the city of Trent (Austria-Hungary) where he worked for the Socialist Party and edited the Socialist newspaper, *L'Avvenire del Lavoratore* ("The Future of the Worker"). During this period, Mussolini also wrote for and edited the Socialist newspaper *Il Popolo* ("The People"). His writing for the newspaper included a novel translated into English as the "THE CARDINAL'S MISTRESS". The novel was intended to degrade the Catholic Church. (Mussolini was anti-Catholic in his early life though, later, compromises with the church were instrumental in his achieving total power.)

Because of Mussolini's anti-clericalism and defiance of royalty, he was deported back to Italy. He took a job on the staff of the "Central Organ of the Socialist Party," *Avanti!* (Italian newspaper)|*Avanti!* ("Forward!").

When the issue of Italy entering the FIRST WORLD WAR arose, a group of former Socialists (during this period, Italian Socialists were pacifists) founded the *"Fasci d'azione rivoluzionaria internazionalista"* in October 1914. Mussolini left the Socialist movement and joined the "Milan Fascio" when the FIRST WORLD WAR started. This was against the Socialist principle of pacifism and resulted in the Socialist party expelling Mussolini. After being expelled, Mussolini started his own newspaper, "THE PEOPLE OF ITALY". The newspaper supported the entry of Italy into the war on the side of Britain and France. Mussolini did not want Italy left out of what he called a grand drama. In 1915, Italy entered the war on the side of England and France as Mussolini advocated.

Mussolini joined Italy's prestigious Bersaglieri Regiment as a private, seeing some combat. He spent about 2 years in the military and was injured during hand grenade practice. Discharged, he returned to his newspaper in October 1917. Publishing his "DIARY OF WAR" enhanced his reputation. His newspaper's editorial policy supported the war. In a complete change from his earlier Socialist – Pacifist stance, Mussolini called the parliamentary democracy "effete". As a solution, he advocated a dictatorship.

A deep economic depression occurred in Italy at the end of WORLD WAR ONE. Economic recovery required stability and repeated strikes by Communist and Socialist controlled labor unions coupled with threats of seizure of private property by local governments or gangs of local thugs stymied any attempt at recovery. Both the Communists and Socialists recognized that the destruction of the economy was necessary to allow them to gain power but their efforts only succeeded in aiding Mussolini.

The economic chaos was the most important aid to Mussolini's quest to become a totalitarian dictator. The cornerstone of his movement had been laid.

In March 1919, FASCISM became an organized political movement. Mussolini's party was called the *Fasci di Combattimento* (Combat Group). The "COMBAT GROUP" was supported by a veteran's group named the "ARDITI" (from *ardito*, meaning brave). The "ARDITI" were organized in many Italian towns to initiate violence against those they considered traitors. Together, the two groups formed the base for Mussolini's infamous "BLACK SHIRTS". (The "BLACK SHIRTS" were the Italian version of Hitler's "BROWN SHIRTS") The "BLACK SHIRTS" were a well armed militia controlled by Mussolini and funded by wealthy industrialists and landowners. After Mussolini obtained power, the "BLACK SHIRTS" were integrated into the secret police.

The Fascists failed miserably in the 1919 elections, because they concentrated on foreign affairs. However, Mussolini soon adopted a more popular agenda and it was only a matter of time until the blatant use of force by Mussolini's Militia destroyed all organized opposition and gave him dictatorial power.

A sore loser in the election of 1919, Mussolini's private militia threw bombs at a Socialist victory parade and mailed bombs to opposition leaders. This was one of the few times the government moved against Mussolini's use of force, but he spent only a few days in prison for the offense.

In the summer of 1920, waves of strikes shut down industry and mobs of demobilized soldiers were overrunning estates and seizing land. Local elections gave Socialists and Populists control of local governments. Landowners, farmers and shopkeepers joined together to protect their interest, and with national government approval hired groups of Fascists. The Fascist crushed the opposition but conflict between management and labor continued and the government forced compromises that were resented by the industrialists. The humiliated industrialists turned to the Fascists for help.

Mussolini's financial support increased. He abandoned many of his less popular stands and endorsed a popular agenda that appealed to his new constituency. The Socialists and Communists provided the enemy that all "WANNABE PEERS" must use to obtain power.

A period of relative calm prevailed but Mussolini continued to attack the Socialists and Communists with both rhetoric and violence. His street thugs (BLACK SHIRTS) were better armed and more agressive than the opposition. They destroyed the opposition's newspapers, homes and party headquarters. The trade unions were severely weakened. The government failed to fulfill the basic function of protecting the individual or groups of individuals from the initiation of physical force and the "BLACK SHIRTS" took full advantage of the government's failure. Mussolini's Militia and the Socialists – Communists fought for control of the streets. The government remained neutral and the Fascists won. It is not necessary for the government to initiate the use of force against the individual to destroy freedom. It is only necessary for the government to fail to protect the individual from the initiation of physical force to allow the "WANNABE PEERS" to achieve their objective of a totalitarian control.

Once Fascists achieved virtually unrestricted use of force against the opposition, it was only a matter of time until they could seize or usurp the power of the government.

CHAPTER FOUR

Did you ever wonder why the "WANNABE PEERS" advocate the disarming of the citizens in spite of the overwhelming evidence that the policy leads to increased crime and violence? They know that force and threats of force against the individual is necessary to destroy your freedom. Those threats and violence are best implemented by street gangs such as Mussolini's "BLACK SHIRTS" with the tacit approval of government inaction. Such action against an armed citizen is both dangerous to the aggressor (political thugs in the service of "WANNABE PEERS" seeking to expand their power by the use of physical force.) and can result in death and carnage in the streets. The citizens won't tolerate that type of violence. It is absolutely necessary to disarm the citizens to empower the political thugs.

From a few hundred members in 1919, Mussolini's Fascists grew to around 250,000 in 1921. The Fascist won 35 of 535 seats in the 1921 elections and Mussolini became a Member of Parliament. Because of the large number of political parties winning seats and the dissention between parties, the forming of a government was difficult and governmental authority was severely limited. Due to this fragmentation, the Fascists became a member of the ruling coalition. By withdrawing their support, the Fascists were able to topple the government. Twice new governments were formed excluding the Fascists but the newly formed governments were ineffective. Mussolini's promise of restoring Italian power and prestige, reviving the economy, increasing productivity, ending harmful government controls and restoring law and order were a stark contrast to the ineffective government provided by the loose coalition in power. Mussolini's message was a very popular if somewhat false statement.

The contest for control of the government was between the Fascists and the Socialists-Communists. There was no faction that advocated individual freedom (Capitalism). All that was to be resolved was the nomenclature of the totalitarian government. It was only a matter of the identity and title of the Dictator.

The Fascist control of the streets made a coup inevitable. The opposition was severely weakened by the "BLACK SHIRTS" aggressive and violent acts. The Socialist and Railwaymen's Union tried to stop the Fascists by declaring a general strike. The armed Fascists broke the strike by stepping in and providing the essential services. The strike lasted less than four days and the Fascists won the support of the middle classes.

By October, 1922, the Fascists, emboldened by their monopoly on force in the streets, planned a march on Rome to force a coup. The government finally recognized that the "BLACK SHIRTS" violence was a threat to the government and tried to implement martial law to protect the government. A Declaration of Martial Law required the signature of the King and the King refused to sign the declaration. To prevent a civil war, the King tried to create a coalition government excluding the Socialist and Popular Parties. Even though the Fascist only controlled 35 seats, Mussolini refused to participate unless he was to be the Prime Minister. Faced with a choice between the Fascists, the Socialist-Communists or a civil war, the King chose Mussolini to form the government. Mussolini became the Prime Minister and the threatened Fascist march on Rome became a victory parade. The victory parade took place between October 27 and October 29, 1922.

Mussolini now controlled the government even though the Fascists controlled less than 10% of the 535 seats in parliament. Now it was only a matter of consolidating his power. With the opposition crushed, a period of relative stability and prosperity ensued. A combination of prosperity, physical force against the opposition and virtual total control of the media, Mussolini's party won 374 seats in the Parliament in the April 1923 elections.

Flush with victory, Mussolini's secret police, the "Cheka", physically attacked anyone hostile to Fascist interest and even kidnapped and murdered a popular Socialist leader. The murder caused some popular dissention but only proved to be a minor disruption in the consolidation of Mussolini's power.

Hostile newspapers were shutdown, labor unions were crippled, agreements with all powerful interest were made and Mussolini was in total control.

The Italian dictatorship preceded Germany's Fascist coup by ten years.

ADOLF HITLER[16]

Adolf Hitler, a hero or a villain? King George III and his "PEERS" would have lusted after his exercise of total power. Thomas Paine would have recognized Hitler as the

92

legacy of KING GEORGE III and a threat to individual freedom and prosperity. He would have been amazed at citizens exchanging their freedom for promises of prosperity and retaliation against a vilified enemy. To Thomas Paine and anyone who believes in individual freedom, Hitler was pure evil.

Over 60 years after his suicide in an underground bunker in Berlin with Russian troops less than 300 yards away and advancing, Adolf Hitler's name still invokes strong emotions. Most understand the death and destruction caused by his totalitarian dictatorship. Some still advocate his racist agenda and endorse his concept of a totalitarian form of government.

How did Hitler destroy an industrial democracy and create a totalitarian government? The economic conditions and Hitler's tactics were very similar to those used by Mussolini. If it could happen in Germany and Italy, it can happen here. Some would say that it is already happening here. We must be able to recognize the tactics and conditions that produced the coup in those two countries if we are to retain our freedom. So let's see how Hitler came to power. (Note 16 in the bibliography lists the research that is the basis of the following analysis)

The tactics and plan that achieved the totalitarian government in Germany were almost identical to those used by Mussolini to take control of Italy. Mussolini came to power ten years before Hitler so Hitler's successful coup was almost a reenactment of the Fascist coup completed earlier in Italy.

Born on April 20, 1889, in Austria, Adolf Hitler's father was Alois Hitler (an illegitimate son whose mother's name was Schicklgruber). Alois Hitler was a minor customs official. Adolf Hitler's mother was Klara Polzl, Alois's niece and third wife. Alois took the name Hitler (a minor change from his stepfather's name) and Adolf was legally born with the surname Hitler. Some sources relate a troubled childhood with his father violently abusing both him and his mother.

Hitler was a good student in elementary school but after elementary school, conflicts with his father caused rebellion and poor academic performance. His father died in 1903 but his academic performance failed to improve and he did not graduate from high school. In early life, Hitler's ambition was to become an artist. The "ACADEMY OF FINE ARTS VIENNA" rejected his application twice citing "unfitness for painting" as the reason. For a time he became interested in architecture but the lack of technical education prevented him from pursuing a career in that field.

Support from his mother until she died in 1907 and small inheritances allowed him to pursue an art career in Vienna. He ran out of money and was forced to live in a homeless shelter for a period. Though he claims to have had his anti-Semitic views very early in life, a noble Jewish house often invited him for dinner and he used Jewish merchants to market his paintings during his early life.

Hitler served in the 16th Bavarian Reserve Regiment in the FIRST WORLD WAR. As a runner, one of the most dangerous jobs on the front lines, he was often exposed to enemy fire. Discharged with the rank of Gefreiter (equivalent to a Lance Corporal in the British army), he was a decorated soldier, receiving both the "FIRST AND SECOND CLASS IRON CROSS" and "WOUND BADGE".

Still in the army in 1919, working with army intelligence, Hitler was assigned to investigate the "GERMAN WORKERS PARTY". Infiltrating the group, his spirited denunciation of Jews, Marxist internationalism, the Social Democratic leaders of the Berlin government and the "November Criminals" (those he held responsible for Germany's surrender in "WORLD WAR ONE") won his acceptance. The founder of the Party invited Hitler to join the Party, consisting of 55 members at that time, and Hitler was appointed to the executive committee. The Party changed its name to the "NATIONAL SOCIALIST GERMAN WORKERS PARTY".

Even though he was discharged from the army in 1920, his former superiors encouraged him to participate full time in the party's activities. Hitler's oratory flourished and soon he was speaking to large crowds in Munich. A revolt aimed at limiting Hitler's power in the Party failed and he used the incident to enhance personal control of the party. Because of his success, at a Party gathering on July 29, 1921, Adolf Hitler was introduced as "FUHRER" (leader) of the "NATIONAL SOCIALIST WORKERS PARTY", for the first time. Hitler's "beer hall" oratory was responsible for Party growth and he was accepted into the cream of Munich society. Many of those who would be prominent in the Nazi Government joined the Party around this time.

CHAPTER FOUR

According to a German police report, the "NATIONAL SOCIALIST WORKERS PARTY" had grown to 50,000 by the summer of 1923.

The terms of the treaty ending World War I were always one of Hitler's grievances. He constantly denounced those in the German Government who surrendered to the Allies. Germany was late delivering coal (connected with the reparations required by the treaty) to France and France and Belgium invaded the Ruhr. The treaty of Versailles had limited the German army to 100,000 so Germany could not contest the invasion. The invaders established check points in town squares and railroad hubs. The check points were armed with machine guns. They took over customs, railroads and other transportation routes. Germany's most productive industries were shut down by strikes. The inflation, already caused by the excessive printing of money, accelerated with production facilities becoming inactive and caused wide spread destruction of individual wealth. Currency became almost worthless. Those on fixed income lost their livelihood and all savings (money) were rendered worthless. The economic devastation produced an ideal situation for revolution.

Sturmabteilung (SA):

Perhaps the single most important element in Mussolini's rise to power was the use of a paramilitary group called the "BLACK SHIRTS" to terrorize and destroy the opposition. Of course, it was necessary to demonize the opposition before the public would stand for this use of brute force. The NAZI equivalent to Mussolini's "BLACK SHIRTS" was named the

"Sturmabteilung", ("STORM TROOPERS" or "BROWN SHIRTS"). The "STORM TROOPERS" took their name from elite units in the German army in WWI that were roughly comparable to our "SPECIAL FORCES".

Even before Hitler joined the "GERMAN WORKERS PARTY", a group of thugs were used to maintain order at meetings and discourage dissention. As early as October 16, 1919 the thugs ejected hecklers from a Hitler speech. According to reports of the incident, the agitators "flew down the stairs with gashed heads". On February 24, 1920, the thugs again ejected hecklers from a mass meeting. Of course, they could hardly be blamed for maintaining order in their meeting. After all, the hecklers were attempting to use force to disrupt the meeting. Those used to maintain order at this meeting became the basis for the paramilitary arm of the "NAZI PARTY" party. The group became known as "Saalschutz Abteilung" (Hall Defense Detachment), and was now a permanent part of the Party. The "Hall Defense Detachment" would soon be used to disrupt functions of the "Social Democrats" and "Communists". Eventually the "Saalschutz Abteilung" (Hall Defense Detachment) would evolve into the dreaded "STORM TROOPERS" the "SS".

Mussolini's "BLACK SHIRTS" were rarely concerned by interference by the government. Not so, in Germany. Hitler felt it necessary to rename the group the "Turn- und Sportabteilung" ("Gymnastic and Sports Division") to avoid government intervention. But by September 1921 the thugs were informally called the "Sturmabteilung" (SA). The Munich Hofbrauhaus was the scene of a public meeting of the "NAZI" Party in November 1921 and Hitler's speech was disrupted by hecklers. Order was restored by a small detachment of SA. The NAZIS named the melee the "Saalschlacht" (Meeting Hall Battle). The "Saalschlacht" became part of the SA lore and in time became a legendary part of its history. The SA officially became the *Sturmabteilung*.

THE HITLER PUTSCH (BEER HALL PUTSCH) November 8, 1923:

One year earlier than Hitler's failed coup, Mussolini consolidated his power with a "VICTORY MARCH" on Rome. The NAZI PARTY had copied the Italian Fascist in appearance and proposals. Hitler was emboldened by:

- The rapid growth of the NAZI PARTY
- Economic crisis caused by the French occupation of the Ruhr
- Assimilation of many independent groups into the Party
- Support of a popular war time General
- The clandestine support of Bavaria's de facto ruler along with army and police leaders.

Could Hitler replicate Mussolini's coup? No, Germany was not ready for a dictator. On November 8, 1923, Hitler, at the head of the SA, took control of a public meeting held by Kahr, Bavaria's de facto ruler. At gunpoint, Hitler demanded the support of the local military and police for his newly formed government. The military and police were to be used for the destruction of the Berlin government. As soon as he was free of the coercion, Kahr withdrew his support and ordered the police to oppose Hitler's attempted coup.

The next day, sure of the support of the Bavarian military and police, Hitler and the SA started the march from the beer hall to the Bavarian War Ministry where they planned to seize control of the Bavarian government as the start of the "MARCH ON BERLIN".

There was no support. Instead the police dispersed the march and killed sixteen of the marchers. Hitler fled, but was arrested, convicted of "high treason".

The "Hitler Putsh" proved to be just a delay to Hitler's plans. Instead of ending his political career, the trial provided a public forum and publicity for Hitler's political agenda, an agenda that proved extremely popular with the German public. Although Hitler was convicted and sentenced to five years in prison, he was released on December 20, 1924 after serving less than 14 months (including remand). While incarcerated, he dictated the book "Mein Kampf" to Rudolf Hess.

The political and economic conditions had improved while Hitler was in prison adversely affecting the popularity of his message. The failed coup had given Hitler national recognition but also resulted in a ban on the NAZI PARTY in Bavaria.

Hitler succeeded in having the ban removed on February 16, 1925 by promising that the party would not use illegal means to gain power. Even though the party was reinstated, Hitler was banned from public speaking because of an "inflammatory speech".

CHAPTER FOUR

The NAZI PARTY'S major support was concentrated in Munich. A program to extend support throughout Germany was successful and in the process, Hitler again enhanced his personal control of the party.

The "TREATY OF VERSAILLES" had forced Germany to accept all the blame for WWI. The treaty cost Germany some of her territory, her colonies, and obligated her to pay reparations totaling 132 billion Marks. Hitler's message condemning the treaty and blaming it on the "Weimar System" (the current German government) and Jews was well accepted by the public but with the improved economic conditions, the support for the Fascists declined. The NAZI PARTY dropped from 6.5% of the vote in 1924 to 2.6% in 1928. It would take another financial crisis to bring the NAZIS to power.

A new economic crisis developed in 1930. The "GREAT DEPRESSION" hit Germany. The government fell and the NAZIS support surged. Election results indicated that their share of the vote increased from 2.6 to 18.6 percent of the vote and the NAZIS became the second largest party in the Reichstag (Germany's parliament) with 107 seats.

The election resulted in a minority government which required "emergency decrees" by the President to govern. Just as in Italy, the Reichstag was too fragmented to function. The new government policies failed to improve economic conditions and Hitler blamed all Germany's problems on the "TREATY OF VERSAILLES", Jews and the politicians who supported the treaty. Hitler promised to restore prosperity and his message of blame and promise of prosperity were well received.

Hitler ran for President but lost the runoff election in April, 1932 receiving 35 percent of the vote.

The government fell in May 1932. The President appointed a new chancellor and an election was held in July 1932. The NAZIS won 37.4 percent of the vote and 230 seats, becoming the largest party in the Reichstag. The President tried twice to appoint a new Chancellor but both attempts tried to form a new government without the Fascists and failed. Unable to form a government without the NAZIS, the President was forced to appoint Hitler the new Chancellor. Hitler became Chancellor of Germany in January 1933. Attempts to obtain a parliamentary majority failed and new elections were scheduled for March 1933.

In late February (just before the election) a fire in the Reichstag building was blamed on the Communists. A government decree suspended basic rights, including "habeas corpus" and suppressed the "GERMAN COMMUNIST PARTY" and some other groups. Communist party officials were put to flight, arrested or murdered. The SA used paramilitary force to support the NAZI political campaign. But the force added to use of the government resources for propaganda and anti-communist hysteria failed to give the NAZIS either a majority of the popular vote or a majority in Reichstag. The NAZIS won 43.9 percent of the popular vote and 288 seats in the Reichstag.

Having failed to obtain a parliamentary majority in the election, Hitler recognized the impossibility of governing without a majority in the Reichstag. The NAZIS proposed the "ENABLING ACT"[40]. The "ENABLING ACT" gave the cabinet legislative power for a period of four years. The "ENABLING ACT" eliminated the need for a parliamentary majority. Since the "ENABLING ACT" conflicted with the Constitution, passage required a two-thirds majority vote of the Reichstag. Negotiations with the "CENTRE PARTY", the third largest party, provided the necessary votes. On March 23, 1933, the Reichstag assembled with SA serving as guards inside the hall. A mob outside threatened the arriving Reichstag Members and screamed slogans to intimidate the NAZIS' opposition. The Communists and some Social Democrats were excluded from the proceedings. Of course, the "ENABLING ACT" passed.

The "ENABLING ACT", coupled with the "Reichstag Fire Decree", was all that was required to create Hitler's legal dictatorship. The NAZIS banned the "Communist Party of Germany", the "Social Democratic Party" and forced all other parties to disband. On July 14, 1933 the NAZI Party was declared the only legal political party in Germany.

A purge known as The "NIGHT OF THE LONG KNIVES" occurred between June 30 and July 2, 1934. Hitler eliminated all those who were a threat to his dictatorship. The President died on August 2, 1934 and with a little political maneuvering Hitler usurped the power of the presidency and took total control of the military. Now, only an external force could remove Hitler from power.

Fidel Alejandro Castro Ruz:

Castro came to power by an armed revolution against a ruling dictator, not by replacing a mixed economy such as occurred in Germany and Italy. It is of interest because both the successful revolution and results are an excellent example of how and why a totalitarian government is replaced by another dictator. It is proof that "absolute power corrupts absolutely"[13]. A new dictatorship is almost inevitable unless there is a benevolent external intervention such as occurred in Germany, Italy and Japan at the end of WORLD WAR II. An exception was the American Revolution. There were attempts to crown George Washington, the most popular of the American Revolution's leaders, a "KING"[18]. George Washington's refusal to accept the crown was all that prevented the Colonies from becoming a Kingdom. History shows that George Washington was indeed a rare individual, refusing absolute power because of his belief in individual freedom.

With time, the totalitarian government becomes so oppressive and the managed economy reduces the standard of living until the only alternative is armed rebellion. The leaders of the revolution always promise freedom and prosperity after the dictator is deposed. However, just as in Cuba, the results are a brutal purge of those involved in the previous regime and those who present a threat to the power of the successful revolutionary leaders. The purge is followed by consolidation of power of the successful leaders of the Revolution. Until the consolidation of power is complete, the excuse is used that freedom and individual liberty must wait until stability is achieved. Of course, the stability is the total authority of the dictator, who usually uses a more benign title, such as President. Once the Dictator has consolidated his power, references to freedom and rule of law are no longer necessary. The opportunity for freedom has been lost. Generally, confiscation and redistribution of wealth by the winners (remember the "by right of conquest" principle) and optimism by the masses produce a brief period of relative prosperity followed by an increasingly oppressive government maintained by brute force. The revolutionary cycle starts over.

Fidel Castro was the son of a wealthy plantation owner. Though he was 15 years old when his mother and father were married, he was recognized as a legitimate son. During the University years, Castro was a member of the "PARTIDO ORTODOXO", a political party. The "PARTIDO ORTODOXO" exposed governmental corruption, advocated government and social reform, Cuban nationalism, economic independence, freedom from domination by the United States and an end to domination of Cuban politics by the "elite". Reports indicate that he was involved in many violent incidents (some involving murder) during his years as a student.

After practicing law for about three years, Castro instigated an armed insurrection with an attack on the Moncada Military Barracks. The attack failed and resulted in Castro's imprisonment. Serving two years, he was exiled to Mexico where he continued to plot the Revolution. The movement was named the "26$^{\underline{TH}}$ of July Movement" (the date of the attack on the Moncada Military Barracks). Castro's strategy was based upon "guerrilla warfare".

On December 2, 1956, Castro, with 81 revolutionaries, attempted to sneak into Cuba but they were detected by the Cuban army and 20 or less were able to escape into the Sierra Maestra mountains. With aid from the inhabitants, they initiated "guerrilla warfare" against the Batista government. By the summer of 1957, the group had grown to over 800 men. Castro succeeded in getting favorable publicity in the United States. To aid in his propaganda, Castro signed the "MANIFESTO OF THE SIERRA MAESTRA". The "MANIFESTO" promised to restore the "Constitution of 1940" and hold free elections within 18 months of attaining power.

The promise of freedom and prosperity with an information program demonizing Batista gave Castro the support of many of the Cuban people and left Batista with little popular support. Initiated in May of 1958, a Batista offensive to destroy Castro's forces failed miserably, due to the lack of popular support and training of Batista's troops. On the first day of 1959, Batista fled and Castro seized power.

Few of the promises of the "MANIFESTO OF THE SIERRA MAESTRA" were ever implemented and we are still waiting for the free election. As one would predict, a brutal purge ensued. Batista's henchmen and all who posed a threat to Castro were eliminated or neutralized. As do most revolutions, the Cuban revolution resulted in changing one slave master for one even more oppressive. There was no George

Washington in charge of the "26TH of July Movement" and a totalitarian government was inevitable.

Castro, using the preponderance of propaganda and brute force maintained his dictatorship until his health failed and he passed the power on to his brother. As of 2009, the brutal regime still maintained power.

Left unchecked, the "WANNABE PEERS" will destroy our prosperity (if they haven't already completed that phase) and seize totalitarian power. We will live under the same oppression, tyranny and ultimate disaster that characterized the totalitarian governments of the Twentieth Century Dictators. If that happens, there will be no United States to save the world.

Those who seek to regain the power and prestige of KING GEORGE III"s "PEERS" recognize that their greatest obstacle is prosperity and freedom of the individual from the initiation of physical force. Their greatest needs are the ability to control the "preponderance of the propaganda" and a constituency that accepts and fears the designated "enemy".

Economic collapse, initiation of physical force against the opposition, near total control of propaganda and the ability to demonize the designated "enemy" were the key to power by both Mussolini and Hitler. If we are to remain free, we must recognize and defeat these tactics.

CHAPTER FIVE

THE "WANNABE PEERS", THEIR STRATEGY AND TACTICS

A "WANNABE PEER" is a person or group that believes it has the moral right and duty to use the government's monopoly on force to affect social change or even to use that power for their personal benefit. This belief probably has its roots in the doctrine of "THE DIVINE RIGHT OF KINGS"[30] which promotes the idea that some of us possess greater intelligence and are morally superior to the masses. Being morally superior and possessing such enhanced intelligence, the "WANNABE PEERS" believe that it is both their moral duty and right to control the inferior masses and ensure that the wealth, created by the "COMMONS", is put to the "best use". The "best use", of course, is that use selected by the "WANNABE PEERS", often for their own benefit, but with some crumbs left over for the "PAWNS". The "WANNABE PEERS" believe that it is their destiny and duty to prevent the chaos and social injustice that they believe is the inevitable result of individual freedom.

Many of the "WANNABE PEERS" simply want to use the government force to control some aspect of the masses' behavior, such as consumption of alcohol. Those with a limited objective form pressure groups to enact laws to force their ideas on the masses. This group generally becomes the "PAWNS" of the more dangerous of the "WANNABE PEERS", who seek power for the sake of power, control of wealth and personal gain. As the "WANNABE PEER" power increases, their appetite for power increases until their success converts them to "WANNABEE KINGS" and finally to "KING" when their control is complete.

The tactics and strategy described in this chapter have been executed by the "WANNABE PEERS" since before the turn of the Nineteenth Century. Of course, both the tactics and strategy have been upgraded as conditions changed and they observed the successes of foreign despots. The "WANNABE PEERS" of the late Nineteenth and the Twentieth Century were content to slowly increase their power, secure in the knowledge that their superior intellect and moral superiority would prevail. Who could doubt that a more orderly world, free of social injustice, would result from their effort? Of course, as their judgment was substituted for the action of the free market, exactly the opposite occurred, just as any unbiased evaluation of history would predict. The corruption of the free market always creates more problems and those problems are used to justify even more controls. As the "WANNABE PEERS" executed their plan and their power increased, the validity of Lord Acton's quote "Power tends to corrupt; absolute power corrupts absolutely" [13] has been proven. Perhaps this lust for power has already converted some of the "WANNABE PEERS" into "WANNABE KINGS".

The "WANNABE PEERS" always claim a noble motive such as promoting the "common good" or perhaps achieving some religious goal to disguise their real motive. Some may actually believe that their obtaining power will allow them to better serve the common good or some other flawed altruistic goal. The "WANNABE PEERS'" motive may be to enslavement for their personal satisfaction or a belief that they can force happiness and prosperity through the use of coercion. The motive is irrelevant. The eventual results of the loss of individual freedom will be chaos and disaster.

There were "WANNABE PEERS" among the delegates to the constitutional convention[26] in 1797. Alexander Hamilton, one of the "FOUNDING FATHERS", presented a plan for a constitution that featured a Chief Executive, elected for life, with absolute veto power over acts of the legislature. The only difference between Mr. Hamilton's plan and KING GEORGE III'S Monarchy was the method of succession. The Chief Executive proposed by Mr. Hamilton had virtually the same power as that possessed by KING GEORGE III. Mr. Hamilton made many contributions to the American Revolution but it is fortunate that his proposal to the Constitutional Convention[26] was not adopted. His proposal is an example of an intelligent and patriotic individual making a flawed proposal, with the best of intentions.

Who are today's "WANNABE PEERS? Not an easy question to answer and the answer is probably irrelevant. After all, what difference does it make if the "WANNABE

PEERS'" spokesperson is the one lusting after your freedom, a dupe who believes his own propaganda, or merely an actor, with an engaging personality and appearance, hired to sell the "WANNABE PEERS'" latest assault on your freedom. It is the agenda that destroys individual freedom, not personality or intention that defines the "WANNABE PEERS". The loss of individual freedom is the important issue, not the slave master's personality or identity. Don't dwell on the personalities; it makes no difference if the real "WANNABE KING" is the charismatic politician and point man for the distribution of the "preponderance of propaganda" or an old, ugly billionaire who pays the bills and pulls the strings. It is your freedom that is important, not the identity or the intentions of the usurper. The "WANNABE PEERS" can disguise their motives and identity, but they cannot protect their agenda from a careful analysis that strips away the "preponderance of propaganda" and exposes the consequences of their agenda. The motive or real identity of those who seek power to control the individual is irrelevant. The best of intentions cannot change the results.

Until the late Nineteenth Century, the rapidly growing "technology dividend" produced by the newly available individual freedom and the free land available in the West provided an almost intoxicating opportunity to those freed from thousands of years of oppression by the "KINGS". Most Americans were too engaged in creating wealth and enjoying that wealth to seek political advantage over their neighbor; an exception was the confiscation and redistribution of the land controlled by the

Native Americans and Mexico. Both of these activities were an extension to the medieval concept of the principle of "by right of conquest" and facilitated the accumulation of wealth by many fortunate citizens. The destruction of the Native American culture and the ceding of land originally controlled by Mexico to the United States were historical changes.

The destruction of the Native American Culture was probably only hastened by the use of force and confiscation of the Indian land. The quality of life and standard of living offered by the compounding of the "technology dividend" would have caused the Native American to forsake the "hunter – gatherer economy" within a few generations. The confiscation of land and oppression of the Native American left them in poverty and bitter for generations. Even today, the Native Americans have not recovered from the oppression and achieved their rightful place in society.

The acquisition of the land controlled by Mexico could easily be justified because it freed the citizens from a corrupt and oppressive government. The Mexican Government was even more corrupt and oppressive than that of KING GEORGE III. An oppressive and corrupt government that maintains its power through the use of physical force has no moral right to continue in power. Such a government will eventually be toppled by its citizens. Often it is replaced by a new "KING", just as Castro replaced Batista in Cuba. The United States simply provided the benevolent external force that broke the cycle and provided individual

111

freedom in the lands annexed by the United States.

Perhaps the activities concerning Mexico and the Native Americans provided an outlet for the "WANNABE PEERS" who saw the Mexican government and the Native Americans were more vulnerable than the Nineteenth Century "COMMONS".

When the Constitution was adopted, the suffrage[28] was limited to male landowners and the predominant industry was agriculture. There were large plantations, using slave labor, and family farms, some small, some large. The landowner requirement restricted suffrage to the affluent and eliminated a constituency that could be easily duped by the promise of redistribution of wealth based upon political power instead of productivity, thus, eliminating the "WANNABE PEERS'" main constituency.

By the end of the Nineteenth Century, voting rights had been extended and the "Manifest Destiny"[27] had been achieved. The frontier was virtually gone and along with it the free land. With the compounding of the "technology dividend", factories and railroad construction became important sources of jobs and wealth was created at an unprecedented rate. Improved transportation (part of the "technology dividend") facilitated the consumption of products long distances from where the products originated. The "technology dividend" had increased productivity by reducing the labor required to produce the necessities of life. However, the innovation had produced luxuries for ordinary citizens that KING GEORGE III could not have imagined. To acquire these luxuries it was required to maintain the long work hours necessary when the standard of productivity was a farmer and his mule cultivating the forty acres of land.

Even if the frontier remained, "forty acres and a mule" could not provide the standard of living demanded by most citizens at the turn of the Century. Immigration from Europe and the freeing of the slaves had expanded the work force. The new work force (many with little education or job skills) was dependent on jobs and the expanding economy, instead of the frontier.

Many immigrants could not speak the language, few had marketable skills and most of the freed slaves were illiterate, also lacking marketable skills. The freed slaves were the target of discrimination that also inhibited their economic advancement. The spectacular success and opulence of the entrepreneur was a stark contrast to the plight of these "have-nots". In addition to the "have-nots", many of those with a standard of living KING GEORGE III could not have imagined envied the wealth of the successful entrepreneur. Some "PAWNS" were seduced by promises to limit the opulence of the exceptional entrepreneur and redistribution of the wealth created by the most successful of the "COMMONS". Together, these groups (the poor, the victims and envious) formed the nucleus of "WANNABE PEERS'" constituency, the "PAWNS".

It took over 100 years from Cornwallis's surrender before conditions existed to allow the "WANNABE PEERS" to start building a constituency and mount their first attack on individual freedom. The first skirmish in the counterattack of the "WANNABE PEERS" and their first important success was the enactment of the Sherman Antitrust Act[24] in 1890. Still heralded by the "WANNABE PEERS" as a "landmark achievement", it was a law that provided the prosecutors and judges wide latitude in their interpretation of the law. Business practices that achieved efficiency and success could be judged "predatory" and illegal if a prosecutor could get a jury and judge to agree that the practice harmed competitors. Cases were frequently decided upon the effect on competitors (especially when the competitor possessed political clout) rather than the interest of the consumer or society. The most successful "COMMONS", those who had produced and retained considerable wealth, were an easy target. The press termed them "ROBBER BARONS".

Section 1 of the Sherman Antitrust Act lists two types of violations. The first type of violation is a business practice that the Act made illegal, the second type of violation is a business practices that may be illegal, depending on "circumstances", "motive" or "intent". The second type of violation is non-objective and can be applied at the discretion of a prosecutor or bureaucrat for any reason that suits their purpose. The law potentially made any successful business man a criminal at the discretion of the government. Non-objective laws aimed at successful businesses provided the government considerable leverage to control the actions of the most successful citizens. This supposedly anti-monopoly legislation ignores the glaring fact that true monopolies can only exist when supported by government intervention (government force, real or implied).

The three most inefficient and costly monopolies that immediately come to mind are the Post Office, public education and labor unions. Labor unions are included because they are supported by the use of government force and an excellent example of how a monopoly is maintained by government force, real or implied. A union (voluntary association of employees without access to the government's monopoly of force) formed to bargain or initiate dialogue with the employer is simply an exercise of the employees' individual rights and does not constitute a monopoly. The union becomes a monopoly only when it is allowed to use physical force or benefits from the use of force (real or implied) by the government.

With the passage of the Sherman Antitrust Act, the "WANNABE PEERS" became the champion of the "status quo". Prosecution of the most successful "COMMONS" was a drag on the growth of the "technology dividend". Obviously, the company that exploits an invention and causes a competitor's product to become obsolete is engaging in predatory business practice. Just look at the havoc caused to the buggy whip industry by the invention of the automobile. Shameful, why was there no prosecution of the automobile industry? Did the buggy whip manufacturers lack the political clout to get the government protection? With the Sherman Antitrust Act and a little imagination, your streets could still be full of horse manure.

The "WANNABE PEERS'" fortune had changed with the turn of the Century. Their first important victory had been accomplished and they were benefitting from a growing constituency. The "PAWNS" had been created and the class was growing. The campaign to restore the "KINGS'" power and the power and prestige of his henchmen, the "PEERS", was well underway.

The "WANNABE PEERS" were ready to implement the tactics and strategy that could culminate in a coup that would completely reverse the American Revolution. Will the "WANNABE PEERS" give KING GEORGE III the last laugh?

Modern history has many instances of the "WANNABE PEERS" engineering a coup to replace a flawed capitalistic government with a Dictatorship. Those successful coups all involved the following:

- A COMMON ENEMY
- CONTROL OF THE "PREPONDERANCE OF PROPAGANDA" - DISSEMINATION OF LIES AND HALF TRUTHS WITH NO CHANCE OF BEING DISCREDITED
- ECONOMIC CRISES FOLLOWING THE SYSTEMATIC EROSION OF INDIVIDUAL FREEDOM RESULTING IN THE INEVITABLE INCREASE IN POVERTY
- THE USE OF PHYSICAL FORCE (REAL OR IMPLIED) AGAINST DISSIDENTS
- CHARISMATIC PERSONALITY OF THE FUTURE DICTATOR
- PROMISE TO "IMPROVE FOREIGN RELATIONS"
- PATIENCE

Though a tested and proven blue print for the successful coup (replacement of a flawed capitalist system with a dictator) did not exist at the "Turn of the Century", America's "WANNABE PEERS" were able to formulate a workable strategic plan to gain power. That plan has been successfully executed and upgraded for over 100 years. The result has been a slow increase of the "WANNABE PEERS" power, eroding your freedom and inhibiting the growth of the "technology dividend".

THE "WANNABE PEERS'" PLAN:

The development and execution of the "WANNABE PEERS'" plan will be described in the remainder of this chapter. The following chapters will describe the specifics of the progress of their agenda; how the programs were executed, what the "WANNABE PEERS" promised and the actual results.

A COMMON ENEMY:

A basic necessity for a totalitarian government or the "WANNABE PEERS'" is an enemy. Hitler's enemies were the Jews, Communists and Socialists. Mussolini experimented with several enemies, including the church, before selecting the Communists and Socialists. America's "WANNABE PEERS" have declared the enemy to be the "rich". Even the title of the enemy, the "rich", is part of the lie that is supported by the "WANNABE PEERS" control of the "preponderance of propaganda" and an inept opposition. The actions of the "WANNABE PEERS" clearly show that they target only Mr. Paine's "COMMONS" (the producer), not all of the "rich". The "COMMONS" created and retained considerable wealth but their defining characteristic was productivity, not the wealth they accumulated. As the time went on, the "COMMONS'" wealth became the property of their descendants. This transfer of wealth created the "idle rich" (though some of the "COMMONS" heirs continued to be active producers) who had little to do with the creation of the wealth and simply enjoyed the opulence made available by their forebears. It is this "idle rich" class that is resented (falsely) by the general population and taints the word "rich" in many people's mind. The political hacks that accumulated wealth by the use of political favors add even more evil connotations to the word "rich". The political hack class of the "rich" is more of a drag on the economy than the "idle rich".

Both the "idle rich" and the political hacks are the "WANNABE PEERS'" partners. Just as wealthy industrialists were the early supporters and funders of both Hitler and Mussolini, the idle rich and political hacks are the primary source of financial support for the "WANNABE PEERS". The "idle rich" want to maintain the "status quo"; after all, what could improve their station in life? The political hack wants to increase the available plunder by increasing the power of the government. Both of these objectives are compatible.

Of the three classes of the "rich", only one class is the "WANNABE PEERS'" real enemy. That enemy is the innovator, or Mr. Paine's "COMMONS", the creator of wealth. Even with their control of publicity, the "WANNABE PEERS" had to use a term with derogatory connotations to describe their "enemy". The most avid or mentally challenged "PAWN" would reject dialogue that claimed the "PAWN" was being exploited by an innovator or producer. So the "WANNABE PEERS" use the term "RICH" to define their enemy.

Because two classes (inherited wealth and political hacks) of the three classes of the "rich" are the primary financial support of the "WANNABE PEERS", they are excluded from the consequences of being the "WANNABE PEERS'" enemy, even though the "preponderance of propaganda" campaigns may include disparaging statements concerning the "idle rich" and the political hacks (termed "lobbyists" for propaganda purposes). Those opposed to the "WANNABE PEERS" agenda are often called lobbyists. These two classes are the partners of the "WANNABE PEERS'" and benefit from their policies even though they fit most definitions of the term, "rich".

Where is the proof? The graduated income tax is not a tax on wealth. It is a tax on productivity. If "WANNABE PEERS" really wanted to punish the "rich" as they imply, the "WANNABE PEERS'" income tax would be a "net worth" tax (A tax on the individual's "net worth would target all the rich). Fat chance of that; if the "WANNABE PEERS" were to advocate a "net worth" tax their financial support would disappear overnight. The "net worth" tax is just as illogical as an income tax, but depending on the specifics, probably would be less of a drag on the economy.

The sanctions contained in the Antitrust Laws are only applied to the successful "COMMONS" (producer). The "WANNABE PEERS" may call the "rich" the enemy but the actions taken against the "rich" are very selective.

The purpose of the "enemy" is to incite the "PAWNS" emotions causing them to identify with the "WANNABE PEERS" and provide support for proposals which the "WANNABE PEERS" claim will punish the enemy, provide restitution for previous wrongs and prevent the enemy from future transgressions. The acceptance of a common enemy by the "PAWNS" enhances the relationship with the "WANNABE PEERS", strengthening their claim for the future political support of the "PAWNS".

Prosperity born of innovation is the legacy of Mr. Paine's "COMMONS" and prosperity is the scourge of the "WANNABE PEERS". Is it any wonder that the "WANNABE PEERS" chose the "COMMONS" (after relabeling them "rich") as the enemy? The question is how could they have gotten away with it for over 100 years?

The "WANNABE PEERS'" first success, the Sherman Antitrust Act, clearly targets the most productive and successful among us. The harassment or disabling of the producer ("COMMONS") is not in the best interest of the consumer or in the long term interest of the "PAWNS". Standard Oil was convicted of violating the Sherman Antitrust Act after reducing the cost of kerosene from $0.58/gallon to just over $0.07/gallon.

CONTROL OF "PREPONDERANCE OF PROPAGANDA" [29]

The "New World Encyclopedia" defines propaganda as "a specific type of message presentation directly aimed at influencing the opinions or behavior of people rather than providing objective information". That is a very good description of the "WANNABE PEERS" propaganda initiative.

The "WANNABE PEERS" consists of a large group of politicians but to execute an effective "preponderance of propaganda" campaign, they require more than politicians making press releases. A large collection of public figures and pressure groups ("PAWNS" desiring "WANNABE PEERS" support of their specific cause) is necessary to give the illusion of wide spread public support. Most of the support is from sources with close, but not obvious, connections with the "WANNABE PEERS". Of course, the "PAWNS" must have causes that do not conflict with the other "PAWNS" or at least the "PAWNS" must not be aware of the conflicts. To provide the "WANNABE PEERS" effective propaganda, the "PAWNS" must have a good reputation with the media and the public.

The enemy, the "COMMONS", will be blamed for creating and profiting from the problem. The solution will usually punish the "COMMONS" (producer) with rules and regulations that increase the cost of production, increase taxes on the producer and reduce the capital available for expansion increasing the efficiency of production. Of course, the ultimate loser is the consumer.

Press conferences and public interviews are scheduled to start the propaganda surge. Newspapers and magazines run "think pieces" highlighting the injustice, touting the "WANNABE PEERS" solution and the proposed punishment of the "COMMONS". The "PAWNS", dependent on the "WANNABE PEERS" support for political favors and celebrities (eager to show their altruistic values) make similar but not identical statements of support for the issue. All of the participants present only the positive spin on the issue while gloating over the proposed punishment of the "COMMONS".

Generally, popular support for the issue is secured before the opposition even knows it's under attack. How many times have you seen an issue settled or an individual, judged by the "WANNABEE PEERS" to be a threat, demonized by this type of media blitz?

Advancement of the "WANNABE PEERS'" agenda requires that they control the

121

"preponderance of the propaganda". To obtain this control, the "WANNABE PEERS" have to silence the opposition, otherwise the lies and half truths would be exposed. From the late Nineteenth Century to the present, most of their opposition was so inept that silencing it was hardly worth the effort.

How can the "WANNABE PEERS" silence dissidents? Hitler's "Brown Shirts" and Mussolini's "Black Shirts" used physical violence to control public meetings. As their power increased, the thugs destroyed the opponents' property, sometimes even kidnapping or murdering them. However, physical violence in the streets by politically controlled mobs has to wait until the "WANNABE PEERS" achieve considerable power. Of course, politically controlled mobs are not practical with an armed citizenry. Why do you think the "WANNABE PEERS" are so passionate about gun control in the face of all the historical evidence that a disarmed citizen causes increased crime?

There are other methods just as effective as open physical violence and less obvious to the public. The "WANNABE PEERS" use vague laws that permit prosecution for normal behavior. If necessary, the "preponderance of propaganda" initiative can be invoked to vilify and discredit the victim before proceeding with the prosecution. The Sherman Antitrust Act is an example of this type of the "non-objective" type of law that can be used by the government to silence dissent.

Another excellent tactic is to establish a bureaucracy that enforces its rules and regulations with the force of law and holds the victim is "GUILTY UNTIL PROVEN INNOCENT".

The IRS, the EPA and other alphabetical monstrosities that have their roots in the "NEW DEAL" are examples of this type of coercion.

These sanctions can be implemented without the knowledge of the public or with public participation by a mature bureaucracy. When necessary, "preponderance of propaganda" is used to vilify the target.

ECONOMIC CRISES FOLLOWING THE SYSTEMATIC EROSION OF INDIVIDUAL FREEDOM AND INCREASE IN POVERTY:

The constituency of the "WANNABE PEERS" is composed of the "PAWNS", the poverty stricken, those dependent upon the government for their job, the elite (those expecting political favors), the idle rich and the political hacks. Increasing prosperity reduces "WANNABEE PEERS" constituency while declining prosperity enhances their constituency.

The majority of poverty stricken is those with limited education and little or no job skills. Their limited productivity prevents them from accumulating any wealth because their income barely covers survival. Many are dependent on government handouts for survival. Any increase in the cost of living simply increases their misery and makes survival more difficult. It also pushes more marginal workers into poverty. Increases in the cost of basic commodities such as energy can easily destroy the standard of living of those close to the poverty line, destroy jobs and force the relatively comfortable into poverty. The net result is to increase the portion of the population dependent upon the government for survival and increase the dissatisfaction of many who are still able to provide for

123

themselves. Of course, when productivity declines due to government action, the "COMMONS" can always be blamed. The poverty stricken is the portion of the "WANNABE PEERS" constituency that is the easiest to increase. Any rules or regulations that limit production, or increases the cost of production, will reduce the creation of the nation's wealth (and increase the cost of living). When the nation's wealth is reduced, it is the poor that are most affected. A slowdown in economic activity throws people out of work and increases the ranks of the poverty stricken. The net result is an increase in the potential constituency of the "WANNABE PEERS".

Since energy is a component in all "consumable assets", an increase in the cost or availability of energy is the easiest and most effective way to disrupt the economy.

The "WANNABE PEERS" know that increasing their constituency is vital in their quest to increase their power. It is evident from their agenda that the "WANNABE PEERS" know that prosperity reduces their constituency and poverty increases it. The proposals and programs that the "WANNABE PEERS" have successfully enacted show a clear hostility to prosperity. Their programs will either destroy wealth or inhibit the creation of wealth. This assertion will be proven by analyzing the results of many of these programs in the next few chapters.

History clearly shows that an economic crisis is necessary to seize totalitarian power in a flawed capitalistic society. The "WANNABE PEERS" plan has been active for over a century. The series of economic crises and wars of the Twentieth Century have each reduced individual freedom and the following recoveries have not fully restored those freedoms. How much longer can it take to produce the economic crisis that provides the opportunity for the coup that reverses the American Revolution? Laws and bureaucracies now exist that give those in power the ability to control individual dissent. For over a century the basic cost of producing "consumable assets" has been slowly increased by laws, rules, regulations and creative bureaucratic enforcement. These cost increases diminish the "technology dividend" and threaten to totally eliminate it. As one would expect, the "WANNABE PEERS" have benefited by huge increases in their constituency.

These punitive government actions include:

- Creating specifications for "consumable assets" that increase the costs
- Restrictions on harvesting of natural resources
- Meddling in the relationship between employee and employer
- Creating bureaucracies which enforce their regulations on a "guilty until proven innocent" basis
- Non-objective laws that permit indiscriminate prosecution of the "COMMONS" and the protection of the "status quo"
- Intimidation of dissenters with threats of prosecution
- Restrictions on creation of new "active assets" (new production facilities) which

  significantly increase the cost of
  innovation

- Inflation of dollar

     For over a century these ill advised
programs have stifled innovation and increased
the cost of living. The successes of these
programs threaten to spawn the first "retro-
generation" in our nation's history. A
contraction in the economy is sure to produce
an economic crisis allowing the "WANNABE PEER"
to increase the government's power over the
individual. Eventually one of these economic
crises will provide the opportunity for the
coup that reverses the American Revolution.

THE USE OF PHYSICAL FORCE (REAL OR IMPLIED)
AGAINST DISSIDENTS:

     Both Hitler (Brown Shirts and later the
SS) and Mussolini (Black Shirts) used
paramilitary goons to control the activities
of their political opponents. As they gained
power, the use of physical force became more
blatant. Once they gained control of the
government police function, the need for
restraint was removed and the murder and
imprisoning of political foes were commonplace
and there was little or no effort made to
disguise the crimes.

     America's "WANNABE PEERS", so far, have
been unable to use actual physical force
against political opponents. However, they
have been successful in passing "non
objective" laws such as the Sherman Antitrust
Act that allow prosecution based upon the
"motive" or "intent" of the alleged
perpetrator. Any successful "COMMON"
(producer) can be prosecuted under this law
(and later amendments to it) or the law can be

CHAPTER FIVE

used to interfere and cause costly delays in
the implementation of business decisions.

   Complicated income tax laws that are
difficult to comply with, or even understand,
lead to threats of prosecution. Complication,
misunderstanding and ignorance of these laws
lead to prosecutable offenses. Bureaucracies
(the IRS and the EPA are examples) have been
established as investigator, judge, jury and
prosecutor with the power to declare the
victim guilty until proven innocent and punish
the victim with civil fines.

   Both the "non-objective" laws and the
fine levying bureaucracies offer the "WANNABE
PEERS" powerful tools to control dissent and
use intimidation to force support for their
proposals. The more successful the "COMMONS",
the more vulnerable they are to this
intimidation.

   Have these government powers ever been
used by the "WANNABE PEERS" to gain political
advantage? Absolutely; proof is offered in
the succeeding chapters. Such action is
always covert and great care is taken to avoid
its discovery. Chapter 11 has several cases
where the IRS was used to prosecute and
investigate political enemies and the
Bibliography contains the references of many
more cases of abuse. Some years ago there
were reports that a member of Congress
initiated an investigation against the IRS and
just as he came up for reelection, the IRS
charged him with tax evasion and he was
vilified in the press. He lost the election
and the investigation died in the next
Congress. The IRS prevailed and one would
suppose that the IRS activities that the
Congressman was investigating continued. Was

the congressman guilty of tax evasion or the victim of a bureaucratic massacre? Who knows, but the gun is smoking!

This Congressman – IRS incident is a very old memory of the author and considerable research time has been spent (unsuccessfully) trying to verify the information. However, the research uncovered many other "smoking guns" more illustrative of the use of the IRS by "WANNABE PEERS" to intimidate and obstruct political opponents. In Chapter 11 the use of the IRS to intimidate and harass political opponents by Presidents Roosevelt, Kennedy, Johnson and Nixon is discussed. Research indicates that the practice continues today but this book avoids comments of current events that may involve the emotions of the reader and may be lacking in historical proof. Every effort is made to avoid the naming of specific "WANNABE PEERS", and mixing of their personality with the evaluation of the programs. Only those that have passed into history will be mentioned by name. An objective evaluation of the programs demands that the specific personalities and the contemporary "preponderance of propaganda" be separated from the facts.

- The "WANNABE PEERS" have:
- The ability to use the power of the government to intimidate, harass and even destroy "COMMONS" or political opponents
- That power has been used against both "COMMONS" and political opponents

It is later than you think! Only historical examples of the "WANNABE PEERS" agenda and abuses of power are used to avoid the emotion associated with contemporary politicians. The bureaucracies still exist and, if anything, their power has been extended.

When "WANNABE PEERS" and bureaucrats wield the power to prosecute indiscriminately and bureaucrats have the power to levy fines and seize property without due process of the law, exercising your individual freedom becomes a risky endeavor and outright dissent becomes financial suicide. Guilt is irrelevant! Mounting a defense against these powerful bureaucracies can destroy or bankrupt any "COMMON" or political opponent of the successful "WANNABE PEER". It is not necessary for a "COMMON" to be found guilty to be destroyed by this system. An innocent verdict following a bankrupting defense offers little satisfaction.

Intimidation does not require violence in the streets. Powerful bureaucracies and prosecutors, controlled by the "WANNABE PEERS", can be quite effective in their covert actions.

PROMISE TO IMPROVE FOREIGN RELATIONS:

The "WANNABE PEERS" are quick to point out that the United States is held in contempt by the bulk of the world's population and if you look at the media coverage in most countries you will find that their media constantly publishes disparaging articles about the United States. Many of these articles blame the prosperity of the United States for their domestic poverty. The United States has been the most desired location for those immigrating to a new country for many years. Why would so many people want to immigrate to a country they despise? Most people would rather be prosperous than be a victim and the more intelligent know that they are the victim of the "KINGS" and "PEERS" who control their government.

The governments of most countries are dominated by "WANNABE PEERS", "WANNABE KINGS" and "KINGS". These leaders control the "preponderance of the propaganda". They use propaganda to increase and maintain their power while diminishing whatever individual freedom still exists in their countries. The prosperity created in the United States by the near capitalistic system and individual freedom is a severe embarrassment to all those "WANNABEE PEERS" and "KINGS". Public opinion in the countries dominated by these authoritarian rulers is simply a reflection of the way the government uses the "preponderance of propaganda" to discredit the success of the near capitalist system in the United States.

The claim by the "WANNABE PEERS" that their agenda will improve the reputation of the United States in those countries dominated by "KINGS" and "WANNABE PEERS" may be true in the short run. If our prosperity and our freedom are destroyed, the United States will no longer be an embarrassment to the leaders of those countries that have never experienced near capitalism. The reputation of the United States might well improve temporarily with foreign masses. However, without a strong capitalistic country to protect itself and its friends, the world would soon degenerate into a "by right of conquest" free for all and all humanity would suffer.

Is sacrificing our freedom and prosperity worth gaining approval of the world's despots? Hardly!

PATIENCE:

Patience is the defining characteristic of the "WANNABE PEERS'" plan. We are into the second hundred years of execution of their plan. Both Hitler and Mussolini tried to push their ascension faster than the conditions would allow and were set back and spent time in jail as a result.

Since their initial success, marked by the passage of the Sherman Antitrust Act, government controls over the economy and the individual have slowly increased. The inflation of the Twentieth Century is proof of their success. Occasionally, the rate of growth has slowed and even some temporary, short lived setbacks have occurred. The repeal of Prohibition is an example. Another example is the reduction in the top rate for progressive income tax in the 1980's. The controlled substances laws soon made the excesses caused by prohibition laws pale in comparison. Changing the maximum rate of the income tax can hardly be classed as rejecting the faulty premise on which the law was based. The "WANNABE PEERS" soon began to raise the top rates.

The rate of destruction of wealth is expanding every day. The patience and perseverance of the "WANNABE PEERS" is pushing us ever closer to the eventual economic crisis that will destroy the last vestiges of capitalism and allow a "WANNABE PEER" to achieve "KING" status.

A SUMMARY - THE "WANNABE PEERS" STRATEGY:

• Obtain control of the "preponderance of propaganda"
• Create and vilify an enemy

131

- Establish means to intimidate and control dissenters
- Establish coalition of "PAWNS" (pressure groups) from those who consider themselves victims and want restitution and vengeance, those who want to use government force to control other's behavior and those who would use government for personal gain
- Institute policies that increase the "WANNABE PEERS" core constituency (those living below the poverty level and dependent on the government for survival)
- Create a series of economic crises that result in incremental loss of individual freedom and eventually resulting in a coup that establishes a "KING"

A SUMMARY OF THE "WANNABE PEERS" TACTICS:

- Gain control of main stream media
- All comments and articles on a subject must be consistent but not identical. All propaganda should reinforce preceding efforts and hold the selected enemy responsible
- Select and vilify the enemy. All "preponderance of propaganda" effort should not only sell the proposal but should reinforce the campaign against the enemy
- Establish non-objective laws to intimidate dissenters
- Create bureaucracies with the power to enforce their rules and regulations on a "guilty until proven innocent" basis (Very effective in silencing dissenters)
- Disarm the citizens (gun control)

- Establish programs with rewards for the "PAWNS" to obtain their support to build a coalition of pressure groups
- Create victimless crimes to reward "PAWNS" whose agenda is behavior control (victimless crimes destroy wealth and provide a mechanism for intimidating dissenters). Enforcement of victimless crimes destroys wealth and causes disruption of the economy
- Make and implement proposals to provide restitution and exact revenge to reward the self professed victims
- Behavior control legislation outlaws whole industries. Prohibition of alcohol is a good example. (destruction of wealth)
- Labor legislation that sanctions the use of physical force by the employees to control the employer's facility to force agreement in labor contracts. These coerced contracts increase the cost of "consumable assets" and in extreme cases can destroy whole industries
- Force the use of government regulations instead of the judgment of the employer to select and promote employees
- Obtain control of energy. All "consumable assets" have energy content and require transportation. Increasing the cost and reducing the availability of energy reduces the standard of living and has the potential to destroy the economy (nothing has more potential to increase the "WANNABE PEERS'" core constituency)
- Implement rules and regulations that limit the use of private property without compensation to the property owner.

133

(Limiting the use of the property destroys wealth)

- Limiting the harvesting of natural resources (inhibits the creation of wealth)
- Earmark legislation (deployment of wealth without regard to return on investment is destruction of wealth)
- Inflation of the currency, a covert tax that increases the real wealth controlled by the government. (redeploys wealth to non productive uses, destroys savings which increases the portion of the population dependent on the government for survival)
- Environmental rules and regulations that destroy wealth and increase the cost of living with no return on the investment. (Enhancement of the quality of life is a return on investment and environmental initiatives that maintain and enhance the quality of life are not a part of the "WANNABE PEERS" agenda. Most environmental issues have little, if any, payback and could never pass an "economic impact statement")
- Taxing the "COMMONS" on productivity destroys their ability to generate capital for economic expansion (redeploys wealth from the most productive uses and destroys the incentive of the "COMMONS", a devastating effect on the compounding of the "technology dividend")
- Allow immigration of persons who have no wealth and little or no job skills. (an instant increase in the ranks of the poverty stricken and in the "WANNABE PEERS" constituency)

- Use charismatic spokespersons to sell their programs and disguise their true objectives
- Use extreme patience and take only what the "COMMONS" are willing to give up at any given time, avoid conflicts and evaluations that could expose the real effects of proposals (The only possible conclusion of the slow methodical destruction of individual freedom (capitalism) is the economic crisis that reestablishes the power enjoyed by KING GEORGE III but under new management)

By the turn of the century, the "WANNABE PEERS" had selected an enemy and even applied the first sanctions against that enemy. The counter revolution was well underway and the "COMMONS" had hardly noticed.

The "WANNABE PEERS" can look back on over 100 years of degrading our individual freedom. The ultimate coup is very close. Today, the same peril exists for our freedom that existed when the "Minutemen" stood on Lexington Green[25]. Will descendants of the "SONS OF LIBERTY" remember the "SHOT HEARD AROUND THE WORLD" and turn back this insidious assault on individual freedom?

CHAPTER SIX

THE "WANNABE PEERS" SUCCESSES[49]

The American Revolution destroyed the "PEERS" source of power and prestige and established a new source of power, the ballot box. When the British military evacuated the United States, the Colonists (Tories) who had been loyal to King George III, left with them. Not only had the "PEERS" lost their power; they were physically removed from the United States so Mr. Paine's "PEERS" no longer existed as a class of citizens in the United States. The battle was won, but not the war. The "PEERS" were replaced by the "WANNABE PEERS". The "WANNABE PEERS" are politicians seeking the return of power and prestige enjoyed by KING GEORGE'S "PEERS". The "WANNABE PEERS" devised the strategy and tactics to guide their quest to regain the power and prestige that the English "PEERS" enjoyed at the pleasure of KING GEORGE III. Eventually, perhaps they could even mount a counter revolution and place a "WANNABE KING" on the throne. The source of power would be changed back to the "KING" and the "WANNABE PEERS" would again be real "PEERS" free to use the force of the government to exploit the "COMMONS". The indignity of catering to the "PAWNS" for their vote would be ended.

In the early days, the "WANNABE PEERS" were only concerned with small increases in

136

personal power but small successes only increased the thirst for power.

It took over 100 years from the adoption of the Constitution for the "WANNABE PEERS" to win their first important victory. That victory, the passage of the Sherman Antitrust Act, was the beginning of a successful and very patient campaign to restore the power and prestige to the "WANNABE PEERS". Will they regain the power and prestige enjoyed by the British "PEERS"? Can the "WANNABE PEERS" usurp control of the wealth the "COMMONS" create? Can they regain the power to punish the "COMMONS" who rebelled against their "benevolent coercion"? Perhaps they already have!

Innovation, the "technology dividend", had created huge productivity increases and unprecedented prosperity. If the "WANNABE PEERS" were to increase the ranks of the poverty stricken (their core constituency), innovation would have to be controlled, or even reversed. The "WANNABE PEERS" would be the champions of the "status quo" and recipients of the "PAWNS'" political support.

If successful, the "WANNABE PEERS" agenda would result in an economic crisis severe enough to destroy the last vestige of "Capitalism". The final conclusion would take generations and require considerable patience but the hard core "WANNABE PEERS" had no doubt that their "benevolent coercion" would eventually restore their lost power and prestige.

The issue is still in doubt. We are Twenty-First Century Minutemen, standing on today's "LEXINGTON GREEN" with the "WANNABE PEERS'" army of bureaucrats advancing with rules, regulations and threats of prosecution instead of muskets. If we don't reverse the trend, our freedom will be lost forever!

How have our freedoms been usurped by the "WANNABE PEERS"? We will evaluate the programs that the "WANNABE PEERS" have proposed and executed in the late Nineteenth Century and early to mid Twentieth Century. These historical programs have been in force for many years and ample historical data is available to make a complete evaluation. This approach avoids conflict with the "preponderance of propaganda" that accompanies the introduction of current assaults on our freedom and the emotion associated with current proposals. Since the "WANNABE PEERS" proposals destroy individual freedom, the analysis of the results of the loss of individual freedom has a direct bearing on current proposals. Our purpose is not to pass judgment on the historical figures. The purpose is to show how the results of the "WANNABE PEERS" proposals are opposite those touted in the "preponderance of propaganda" sales job and compound over time to destroy our way of life.

Was a "counter revolution", the destruction of individual freedom and the establishment of an elite autocracy, the conscious objective of all, or any, of those that participated in the passage of the Sherman Antitrust Act and other programs we will evaluate? No. Most of the 293 (there was only one dissenting vote) Senators and Congressmen who voted for the Sherman Antitrust Act probably had no idea of the long term implications of the legislation. Few even considered it an important piece of legislation. Many thought the law was too vague to be enforced. Few politicians start their public life with the objective of becoming a dictator (Adolf Hitler was one). Most "WANNABE PEERS" just want to enhance their personal power and above all, be reelected. Their success proves the validity of the quote "Power tends to corrupt, and absolute power corrupts absolutely"[13]. As history shows, the corruption created by personal power compounds. If left unchecked, the eventual conclusion of that corruption is a totalitarian government.

Many of the "WANNABE PEERS" simply believe their own propaganda and consider themselves serving the public good. Some may really believe that common good would be served by a government controlled by the intellectual elite and consider themselves a member of the club; others simply thirst for the power. A few may even harbor the ambition to become a dictator.

The motives are irrelevant. Motives cannot affect the results of the program and can't excuse erosion of individual freedom and the resulting effect on prosperity. Don't waste time trying to evaluate the "WANNABE PEERS'" objective. If the program destroys freedom; it must be rejected. It is the agenda, not the personality that is important. Whether it usurps just a little freedom or installs a dictator, the strategy and tactics are the same. The destruction of our freedom occurs in small deliberate steps that build on each other until all the chains are in place.

The "WANNABE PEERS" are very close to achieving their objective. Economic crises are becoming more severe and more frequent.

CHAPTER SIX

The control of the media has almost quieted effective dissent. Diminished individual freedom, enforced by bureaucracies with "guilty until proven innocent" power, has provided the "WANNABE PEERS" with another powerful tool to silence dissent. These bureaucracies have increased the cost of doing business, increasing the cost of living and pushed more of the population below the poverty level. Inflation of the currency is increasing at an alarming rate, destroying the value of savings and putting us at risk of hyperinflation[38] such as occurred in Germany in the 1920's.

How did the "WANNABE PEERS" bring the greatest economic engine the world has ever known to the brink of destruction? In less than 200 years, we progressed from sailing ships to space travel. In 1969, man first walked on the moon and today, we are afraid to harvest our natural resources or even take a Sunday drive for fear of destroying the planet. While promising prosperity, the "WANNABE PEERS" have destroyed our capacity to create wealth! How did they do it?

Starting with "WANNABE PEERS" earliest success, the Sherman Antitrust Act, some of the typical programs will be examined and actual results exposed and compared with the results the "WANNABE PEERS promised. The evaluation of each program will include:

- How these programs were sold to the public
- What the announced objectives were
- The actual results

Only programs which have been adopted and enforced long enough to have ample historical evidence of results will be evaluated. The actual results of their programs will be contrasted with the spin used to sell the program, allowing the reader to make an objective assessment of the program.

Be forewarned, this analysis may differ from prevailing public opinion and the "preponderance of propaganda" which only recognize the positive results and ignore any negative results. Once the historical results of the "WANNABE PEERS" agenda is exposed, the spin used to sell new assaults on our freedom will be ineffective.

The "WANNABE PEERS" have almost eliminated innovation, the source of the "technology dividend". Government control of most of the resources available for research and development is directed toward reward of political cronies and providing technical proof that supports the proposals that would transfer wealth to political allies instead of new inventions that create wealth.

Stopping the advance of the "WANNABE PEERS'" agenda will only slow the decay of our economy and way of life. The trend must be reversed to avoid disastrous economic crises that will result in a totalitarian government. The "WANNABE PEERS'" programs, some that have existed for over 100 years, must be dismantled. A successful termination of these old programs will destroy the foundation of the "WANNABE PEERS'" agenda and enacting new initiatives will be impossible. The "WANNABE PEERS'" cannot effectively sell new programs if the foundation is destroyed.

Beware the spin. Remember, it is a rare program that has no redeeming features. Those benefiting from the program will be quick to point out the advantages and the "preponderance of propaganda" will be totally silent on the consequences. Many times the benefits accrue to a small group but the costs are spread over a large group. Those paying the bill don't even realize they are being exploited.

The programs that will be analyzed and exposed are:

- SHERMAN ANTITRUST ACT[24]
- BUREAUCRACIES
- MANIPULATION OF THE MEDIUM OF EXCHANGE (INFLATION)
- EARMARKS
- INCOME TAX

These programs were selected because:

- The programs are representative of the "WANNABE PEERS'" agenda
- Historical accounts, of the results of these programs are available and conclusive
- The "preponderance of propaganda" that sold these programs to the "PAWNS" is long past, so time has dulled the emotions which once ran high on some of these items. The reader should be able to make an intellectual rather than emotional evaluation
- It takes little imagination to apply the lessons learned from studying these programs to the "WANNABE PEERS'" current agenda

CHAPTER SEVEN

SHERMAN ANTITRUST ACT:

THE SALES CAMPAIGN:
The United States changed from a predominately agricultural society to an industrial society in the mid to late Nineteenth Century. This change provided the conditions that led to the Sherman Antitrust Act. Agriculture and small enterprises (mostly family owned) were the primary form of business in the early Nineteenth Century. In 1860, the largest industrial employer in the United States was the Bath Iron Works of Maine[20] with 4500 employees. The immense capital required to create the railroad industry changed the structure of business in the United States. The corporate structure was required to raise the capital necessary to build the railroads. Even the early railroads were corporations.

When the Civil War ended in 1865, there were still few large industrial concerns in the United States. The corporate world was mostly confined to the railroads. The Erie Railroad was chartered in 1832. In the early 1860's Cornelius Vanderbilt, a large owner of commercial ships became interested in the railroad business. Mr. Vanderbilt purchased two local New York railroads and soon merged with several other railroads setting the stage

143

for a decade long struggle between Mr. Vanderbilt and Daniel Drew of the Erie Railroad. The conflict ended with the "Erie Wars"[20] and was marred by stock manipulation and corruption. The "Erie Wars" fueled an initial distrust of Corporate America by the general public and was a big factor in public support for the Sherman Antitrust act.

In the early 1880's a wave of consolidation of industry began. Increases in individual productivity that had been achieved in the early industrial revolution were no longer enough to maintain the economic growth. To continue the economic growth and expand the rate of that growth, the compounding of the "technology dividend" required that industry take advantage of the "economy of scale"[42]. Companies formed "trusts" to obtain capital, consolidate purchases and set prices for their products. Capital investment enabled increased production at a lower cost. To take advantage of the "economy of scale", the "trusts" lowered prices to increase sales. The lower prices, of course, drove the marginal producer out of business. Consumers benefited but the marginal producer, those not taking advantage of improved technology and the "economy of scale", had to find another way to make a living. The "preponderance of the propaganda" blamed the trusts for "predatory" business practices that destroyed their competitors, oblivious of the fact that the additional resources required for production by the inefficient producer is wealth destroyed and a drain on the economy. Reduced cost of production allowed the "COMMONS" (producers) to reduce prices to the consumer and increase market share, enhancing the effect of the "economy of scale", and continuing the cycle. Low prices made possible by the innovation of the more efficient producer were driving the high cost producer out of the market. The owners of the trusts benefited from their innovation and the resulting creation of wealth. The consumer also benefited from the lower prices. The "preponderance of propaganda" concentrated on the business failures (the inefficient producers leaving the market) and the opulent life style of the "COMMONS" (efficient producer). With the negative publicity, the small business man, some academics and many individuals were frightened by the size and power of the trusts. The states enacted laws outlawing trusts but state laws were not effective because a corporation from one state could do business in other states. "WANNABEE PEERS" in Congress, noting the public animosity toward the trusts, sensed that it could be used for political advantage.

Historical evidence indicates that the Sherman Antitrust Act was not the real objective of the "WANNABE PEERS" at the time it was passed. Some believe the real objective was to pander to the public's fear of trusts and divert attention from the passage of the "McKinley Tariff Act of 1890", also known as the "Campaign Contributors' Tariff Bill". The "McKinley Tariff Act of 1890" was generally acknowledged as a pro-trust measure. A New York Times article states the belief that Sherman supported this "humbug of a law" to allow the party to claim that the party had attacked the hated "trusts". The Sherman Antitrust Act was simply deception by the "WANNABE PEERS" to secure the "PAWNS" support.

The success of the large corporations using the "economy of scale"[42] drove many smaller competitors out of business. The opulence of the "robber barons"[44] (a derogatory term used by the press to vilify the very successful "COMMONS") and bad press caused the individual and small business person to fear the power and distrust the "COMMONS". Following public sentiment, in 1890 the Congress passed the Sherman Antitrust act. The "WANNABE PEERS'" first important victory passed Congress with only one dissenting vote.

At the time of the passage, few recognized the significance of the law and most thought it too vague to be enforced. Those who felt safe because they believed that the law could not be enforced failed to recognize the ingenuity of the "WANNABE PEERS" in the pursuit of power. The "WANNABE PEERS" now had an important tool to increase their power over the "COMMONS".

THE PURPOSE OF THE SHERMAN ANTITRUST ACT:
One of the authors of the Sherman Antitrust Act, Senator George Hoar states the purpose:

"Any company that "got the whole business because nobody could do it as well as he could" would not be in violation of the act. The law attempts to prevent the artificial raising of prices by restriction of trade or supply. In other words, innocent monopoly, or monopoly achieved solely by merit, is perfectly legal, but acts by a monopolist to

artificially preserve his status, or nefarious dealings to create a monopoly, are not."

Apparently not all in the Congress agreed with Senator Hoar. During the debate, Representative Mason stated:

"Trusts have made products cheaper, have reduced prices; but if the price of oil, for instance, were reduced to one cent a barrel, it would not right the wrong done to people of this country by the trusts which have destroyed legitimate competition and driven honest men from legitimate business enterprise."

One would hardly recognize that Congressman Mason was talking about the inefficient producer who was wasting the country's wealth. Some recognized that the Act would harm consumers if it reduced the "economy of scale"[42] by breaking up big business and protecting the "status quo".

Compounding the "technology dividend" is not possible when the government uses its monopoly on force to maintain the "status quo".

The earliest use of the Act was an attempt to settle the "Pullman Strike" in 1884. The act was invoked against the "American Railway Union". Court decisions and general inaction delayed the use of the law to harass corporations for over ten years.

That changed in 1902. The "Northern Securities Company"[34] was formed to control more than five large railroads. Stock manipulation used in the formation of the "Northern Securities Company" and the resulting concentration of the control of so many important railroads received considerable bad publicity. In response to the

147

"preponderance of propaganda", the United States Department of Justice filed suit against The Northern Securities Company, on behalf President Theodore Roosevelt. A five to four Supreme Court decision convicted the companies of violating the Sherman Antitrust Act. The trust was broken up and 44 more similar cases were prosecuted in the next seven years.

This was just the beginning. The "muckrakers", an early Twentieth Century term for "investigative journalist", had a field day vilifying the most successful "COMMONS".

Most believed and still believe that the purpose of the "antitrust laws" is to protect the consumer from monopolies and this is often offered as a reason for invoking the law. The "preponderance of propaganda" that precedes high profile prosecutions always promises to protect the consumer and describes the harmful and unfair tactics used by the "COMMONS" against the competition.

The vagueness of the Antitrust Laws, coupled with the control of the "preponderance of propaganda" allows the "WANNABE PEERS" to coerce any successful "COMMON" or obtain support from the "COMMON'S" competitors (prospective "PAWNS"). The prosecution of STANDARD OIL is an example of the application of the ANTITRUST LAWS and the effects of those prosecutions on the economy. Fortunately, for the country, the prosecution of Standard Oil did not occur until the company had developed the innovation and economy of scale to provide an efficient and profitable petroleum industry.

STANDARD OIL-THE "PREPONDERANCE OF PROPAGANDA" ATTACK:

Ira Tarbell[41] and Henry Demarest Lloyd were the source of the "preponderance of propaganda" that eventually resulted in the conviction of "STANDARD OIL" for violating the Sherman Antitrust Act. The conviction resulted in the breakup of the company into 34 new companies. Ms. Tarbell wrote two very derogatory books about Standard Oil:

- "THE RISE OF THE STANDARD OIL COMPANY"
- "THE HISTORY OF THE STANDARD OIL COMPANY: THE OIL WAR OF 1872"

Both books were also published as a series of articles in "McClure's Magazine and were highly critical of the business practice of Standard Oil and vilifying the founder, John D. Rockefeller. Ms. Tarbell emphasized the public's misconception of Mr. Rockefeller and distorted the fact that he had been a Sunday school teacher, with Spartan tendencies, who had achieved success because of a frugal life style, exceptional organization and technological innovation. She highlighted the devastating effect that the company's efficiency had on smaller competitors (the technologically challenged). The advantage of the reduced prices to consumers which resulted from the increased efficiency of "STANDARD OIL" was ignored. Her literary efforts inflamed public opinion against "STANDARD OIL" and were influential in initiating the prosecution and eventual breakup of the company.

Ms. Tarbell could hardly be classified as a "disinterested observer". Competition from "STANDARD OIL" resulted in the failure of her father's business in 1872 and her brother was involved with the "PURE OIL COMPANY" a competitor of "STANDARD OIL".

THE STANDARD OIL COMPANY[33]:

   One of the earliest and most successful of the Nineteenth Century industrial corporations was Standard Oil, founded by John D. Rockefeller[43] in 1870 and he ran the company until he retired in 1897. The success of Standard Oil made Mr. Rockefeller the world's richest man. When he died in 1937, Mr. Rockefeller's net worth was estimated at $1.4 billion. When his fortune is evaluated as a percentage of the United States gross domestic product, it is the largest American fortune ever accumulated. Neither Bill Gates' nor Sam Walton's fortune even come close.

   Mr. Rockefeller's frugal nature would lead to the creation of manufacturing efficiency that his competitors could not or did not match. Examples of these innovations:

- The use of refinery byproducts as fuel for his machinery
- Innovative changes in the shipping of both crude oil and finished products
- Creating markets for refinery byproducts considered waste by competitors
- Vertical integration such as making the barrels to ship finished products
- Capital investment in equipment to increase efficiency
- Self insuring his refineries

   Lower prices enabled by better operating efficiencies increased sales. The large volume resulting from the low prices and innovative shipping techniques allowed Standard Oil to negotiate lower shipping rates than the competition. The competition could not compete with Standard Oil's prices and had to choose between selling out to Standard Oil or bankruptcy. Purchasing of competitors provided Standard Oil with a source of talented executives. Innovation and negotiations of favorable freight rates allowed Standard Oil to reduce the price of a gallon of kerosene from $0.58 in 1865 to $0.26 in 1870, a period of only 5 years. Continuing to fall, the price reached $0.10 a gallon in 1874 and $0.09/gallon by 1880. By 1890, Standard Oil controlled 88 per cent of the refined oil flow in the United States and the price of kerosene reached $0.0738/gallon.

Establishing a "RESEARCH AND DEVELOPMENT GROUP" to maintain its competitive lead was another first in American industry for Standard Oil.

In 1892, the State of Ohio won a suit against Standard Oil ordering dissolution of the trust but the company's creative legal maneuvering prevented the conviction from crippling the company. The growth and efficiency of Standard Oil resulted in the absorption and destruction of their competitors throughout the northeastern United States. Some of the competitors found competing with Standard Oil was futile and became partners with Mr. Rockefeller. In 1874, Standard Oil absorbed "CHARLES PRATT AND COMPANY". Two of the company's principals, Charles Pratt and Henry H Rogers became Mr. Rockefeller's partners. Rogers was a key man in setting up the Standard Oil Trust and Mr. Pratt's son became the Secretary of Standard Oil. Mr. Rockefeller retired in 1897 but his involvement in the company began to decline

much earlier. Success continued but did not
match the earlier success during Mr.
Rockefeller's control. Standard Oil ceased to
engage in price competition and buying up
competitors in 1900. In the early 1900's, the
efficiency advantage of Standard Oil's
refineries had been matched by their
competitors such as ASSOCIATED OIL AND GAS,
TEXACO, SUN OIL AND UNION OIL. In 1899, most
of the refinery output was kerosene and
slightly over half of the kerosene was
exported. The major use of kerosene was to
fuel lamps and between 1899 and 1914 Edison's
light bulbs had made huge gains in the
lighting market, displacing the kerosene lamp.
The refinery output (kerosene declined as a
percentage of refined products while gasoline
increased from 15% to 48%. Standard Oil
dominated in the age of kerosene but the age
of kerosene was over. Oil was a changing
market, with oil discoveries outside the
United States; the market was becoming too
large to be dominated by a single company.

Mr. Rockefeller was consistently
criticized by the muckrakers and the press,
because of his great wealth and unparalleled
success. But some, such as Allan Nevins,
provided a more balanced evaluation.

Allan Nevins[45], one of Mr. Rockefeller's
biographers, made the following statement:

**"The rise of the Standard Oil men to
great wealth was not from poverty. It was not
meteor-like, but accomplished over a quarter
of a century by courageous venturing in a
field so risky that most large capitalists
avoided it, by arduous labors, and by more
sagacious and farsighted planning than had
been applied to any other American industry.**

The oil fortunes of 1894 were not larger than steel fortunes, banking fortunes, and railroad fortunes made in similar periods. But it is the assertion that the Standard magnates gained their wealth by appropriating "the property of others" that most challenges our attention. We have abundant evidence that Rockefeller's consistent policy was to offer fair terms to competitors and to buy them out, for cash, stock, or both, at fair appraisals; we have the statement of one impartial historian that Rockefeller was decidedly "more humane toward competitors" than <u>Carnegie</u>; we have the conclusion of another that his wealth was "the least tainted of all the great fortunes of his day."

Even though the efficiency and growth of Standard Oil resulted in lower prices for the consumer, publicity on the plight of their competitors caused much public animosity toward the company. The fact that during the life of the Standard Oil Company the price of its products declined significantly is rarely, if ever, mentioned by the "WANNABE PEERS".

THE PROSECUTION:

The five to four Supreme Court decision against Northern Securities[34] in 1904 paved the way for prosecution of any successful "COMMON". Standard Oil and Mr. Rockefeller were not strangers to Antitrust Litigation. The State of Ohio had won litigation which required dissolution of the trust in 1892. Through legal maneuvering, Standard Oil was able to maintain effective control of the trust. Mr. Rockefeller was one of the owners of Northern Securities when the landmark case was lost. Responding to the "preponderance of propaganda" from Mr. Lloyd and Ms. Tarbell, the US Department of Justice filed suit against Standard Oil in 1909. The suit alleged that Standard Oil sustained a monopoly and restrained interstate commerce by:

"Rebates, preferences, and other discriminatory practices in favor of the combination by railroad companies; restraint and monopolization by control of pipe lines, and unfair practices against competing pipe lines; contracts with competitors in restraint of trade; unfair methods of competition, such as local price cutting at the points where necessary to suppress competition; [and] espionage of the business of competitors, the operation of bogus independent companies, and payment of rebates on oil, with the like intent."

The Justice Department alleged that the monopoly had existed in *the* past four years:

"The general result of the investigation has been to disclose the existence of numerous and flagrant discriminations by the railroads in behalf of the Standard Oil Company and its affiliated corporations. With comparatively few exceptions, mainly of other large concerns in California, the Standard has been the sole beneficiary of such discriminations. In almost every section of the country that company has been found to enjoy some unfair advantages over its competitors, and some of these discriminations affect enormous areas."

Standard Oil was charged with four alleged illegal patterns:

"Almost everywhere the rates from the shipping points used exclusively, or almost exclusively, by the Standard are relatively lower than the rates from the shipping points of its competitors. Rates have been made low to let the Standard into markets, or they have been made high to keep its competitors out of markets. Trifling differences in distances are made an excuse for large differences in rates favorable to the Standard Oil Company, while large differences in distances are ignored where they are against the Standard. Sometimes connecting roads prorate on oil--that is, make through rates which are lower than the combination of local rates; sometimes they refuse to prorate; but in either case the result of their policy is to favor the Standard Oil Company. Different methods are used in different places and under different conditions, but the net result is that from Maine to California the general arrangement of open rates on petroleum oil is such as to give the Standard an unreasonable advantage over its competitors"

Standard Oil was alleged to have raised prices to its monopolistic customers but lowered the prices to hurt competitors:

"The evidence is, in fact, absolutely conclusive that the Standard Oil Company charges altogether excessive prices where it meets no competition, and particularly where there is little likelihood of competitors entering the field, and that, on the other hand, where competition is active, it frequently cuts prices to a point which leaves even the Standard little or no profit, and which more often leaves no profit to the competitor, whose costs are ordinarily somewhat higher."

The bulk of the government's complaints are directed at actions deemed harmful to Standard Oil's competitors. The reduced cost of petroleum products to customers was ignored. Finally, in the last paragraph the government alleges that the company sometimes charged "excessive prices" where there was no competition. Part of the justification for the Sherman Antitrust Act was to protect the consumer from monopoly pricing. This is often used as the justification for prosecution of the successful "COMMONS", but is rarely the real reason. In the long term, a real monopoly can exist only when backed by force, and the government has the monopoly on force. Prosecution is always triggered by complaints by the "technologically challenged" or inefficient competitors. The consumer embraces the lower prices made available by the "COMMON'S" innovation and usually only complains when the prices unexpectedly increase significantly.

On the floor of Congress, during debate on the Sherman Antitrust Act, Representative Mason's speech implied that one purpose of the law was to protect the marginal producer from competition (but not in those words).

To illustrate the emotional nature of the "preponderance of propaganda" that eventually resulted in the prosecution of Standard Oil, the two quotes from Ira Tarbell's book "THE HISTORY OF THE STANDARD OIL COMPANY"[41] are offered. Ms Tarbell's description of Standard Oil's competitors:

"Life ran swift and ruddy and joyous in these men. They were still young, most of them under forty, and they looked forward with all the eagerness of the young who have just learned their powers, to years of struggle and development....They would meet their own needs. They would bring the oil refining to a

region where it belonged. They would make their towns the most beautiful in the world. There was nothing too good for them, nothing they did not hope and dare"

Ms. Tarbell's description of the entry of Standard oil in the refinery business:

"But suddenly," Tarbell writes, "at the very heyday of this confidence, a big hand [Rockefeller's] reached out from nobody knew where, to steel their conquest and throttle their future. The suddenness and the blackness of the assault on their business stirred to the bottom their manhood and their sense of fair play...."

With such an eloquent argument, can anyone deny that the perpetrator should be punished for destroying the hopes and dreams of these good men? Can anyone deny that the use of superior technology and operating efficiency to produce and sell a product at a lower price than a technologically challenged competitor is a crime? If the two preceding statements are true, then the government must protect the high cost producer and economic progress (the compounding of the "technology dividend") becomes impossible. Since the consumer price for refined oil products had continually fallen since Standard Oil was started, the real purpose of the prosecution could not have been protection of the consumer.

Mr. Rockefeller officially retired from Standard Oil in 1897; however, he continued to be the majority stockholder. After his retirement, Standard Oil's technological advantage over its competitors declined as did its market share. By 1906, its oil production market share declined from 34 to 11 percent even though its production increased. The refining market share also declined but its output also increased. Standard Oil's competitors were no longer the **"ruddy and joyous"** primitive distillery operators described in Ms. Tarbell's book. Standard Oil's competitors of the 1900's were companies with business organizations and technology equal to that of Standard Oil. Even competitors with good business practices and equivalent technology would benefit if a competitor's "economy of scale" were reduced. That is exactly what happened.

On May 15, 1911 the US Supreme Court upheld the decision to break up Standard Oil into 34 independent companies with different boards of directors.

EVALUATION OF THE ANTITRUST LAWS — THE STANDARD OIL PROSECUTION:

The prosecution of Standard Oil was selected to illustrate the fallacy, hypocrisy and injustice of the Antitrust Laws. It is an early and best example of antitrust prosecution. The historical account is complete and it occurred 100 years ago, so the effects are well known and the emotion that accompanied the prosecution has subsided, allowing an objective evaluation by most readers. The Supreme Court decision against "Northern Securities", a transportation company, was the first successful high profile prosecution under the Sherman Antitrust Act and set the legal precedent for the Standard Oil case.

Exactly what was the crime committed by Standard Oil? Standard Oil's "ruinous" monopolistic practices resulted in the company controlling 88 percent of the refinery market and exploiting the consumer by forcing the price of kerosene (the primary product produced by crude oil refiners during this period) to drop from $0.58/gallon in 1865 to $0.0738/gallon (an 87%reduction in price) in 1890. The same technology that reduced the price also increased the quality of the kerosene, reducing the fire hazard and the smoke produced by the lanterns. Of course, Ms. Tarbell's **"ruddy and joyous"** but primitive distillery operators could not compete against the high quality kerosene at such low prices. Undeniably, Standard Oil was guilty of driving the inefficient producer from the market place and compounding the "technology dividend". Alas, Ms. Tarbell's primitive distillery operators were no longer **"ruddy and joyous"**. Hopefully they were free to pursue more productive careers. During the Congressional debate on the Sherman Antitrust Law, Representative Mason made a statement to the effect that reducing the cost of products to the consumer did not right the wrong done by destroying the inefficient producer.

Standard Oil had been found guilty. The right of the inefficient producer to destroy the nation's wealth had been confirmed by the Supreme Court. Standard Oil's success compounding the "technology dividend" has not been duplicated and that success cannot even be approached until the Antitrust Laws are repealed. Fortunately for the country, the prosecution of STANDARD OIL was after the fact. At the time of the prosecution, STANDARD OIL was already in decline and had already made its contribution to the compounding of the "technology dividend".

It is interesting to speculate on the devastating effect on the "technology dividend" if the prosecution of Standard Oil had occurred in the mid 1880's. Would there even be a petroleum industry, as we know it today?

If the purpose of prosecuting Standard Oil was to punish Mr. Rockefeller, it failed. Mr. Rockefeller had retired from the company over ten years before the prosecution began in 1909. After the break-up, he still owned 25 percent of the companies that resulted from the break-up. The value of those shares doubled with the break-up and he was already the richest man in the world. In the mid 1890's Mr. Rockefeller's efforts had become mainly philanthropic. The successes of his philanthropic activities include the funding of the University of Chicago and the Rockefeller Sanitary Commission that eradicated the hookworm disease. Rockefeller gave almost $550,000,000 to charity. Most would consider this a better use of wealth than allowing Ms. Tarbell's "**ruddy and joyous**" primitive distillery operators to continue consuming the nation's wealth; to say nothing of the millions of dollars Standard Oil's efficiency saved the consumer.

Mr. Rockefeller had been the driving force behind the technological achievements that had originally provided the operating efficiency of Standard Oil. When he ceased to be involved in the day to day operations, the technology advantage began to decline and by the time the prosecution began, the competitors had closed the technology gap. At the time of the break-up, Standard Oil's share of the crude oil market was only 11 percent and the market share of refined products had declined to 64 percent. Aggressive pricing and buying competitors had ceased around 1900.

The decree broke Standard Oil into 34 different companies, each with independent boards. Each company was assigned a geographical area. Some of the companies expanded and increased the competition in the oil industry. Exxon and Mobil Oil, two of the companies created by the 1911 decree, merged (the largest merger in American history at the time) in 1999. The resulting company, Exxon Mobil Corporation, became the world's largest corporation based upon market capitalization in 2009. So after 100 years, the "economy of scale" again prevailed. Most of the accounts of the prosecution of STANDARD OIL state that it must have been "right" because no one ever suggested that it be undone. That is just not true; it was effectively undone by the Exxon-Mobil merger.

The successful prosecution of Standard Oil gave the "WANNABE PEERS" a powerful weapon against the "COMMONS". The law was so vague that it could be applied to any successful "COMMON". With manipulation of the "preponderance of propaganda", guilt could be established before ever setting foot in the courtroom. Exploiting one's technological superiority to reduce prices and increase market share had been proven illegal if it harmed a technologically challenged competitor. Even if the "COMMON" won the court case, the defense could cost millions and the defense would distract executives, preventing them from concentrating on the operation of the company. The mere threat of antitrust prosecution would cause most "COMMONS" to bend to the will of the powerful "WANNABE PEER" and the promise of protection for the marginal producer allows the "WANNABE PEERS" a ready source of "PAWNS".

In his essay entitled *Antitrust,* Alan Greenspan made the following evaluation of the long term effects of the Antitrust Laws:

"No one will ever know what new products, processes, machines, and cost-saving mergers failed to come into existence, killed by the Sherman Act before they were born. No one can ever compute the price that all of us have paid for that Act which, by inducing less effective use of capital, has kept our standard of living lower than would otherwise have been possible."

The use of the government's monopoly on force to protect and perpetuate the inefficient producer can only destroy wealth and retard prosperity. The wealth consumed by the inefficient producer is gone forever and will never be available for economic growth. One of the surest ways to create a "retro-generation" is to use the force of government to protect the inefficient producer.

The damage that the Antitrust Laws have done to the United States economy defies imagination. Despite the technological advances and the "COMMONS" of the Twentieth Century, the wealth (when evaluated as a percent of the GDP) created by Mr. Rockefeller remains unequalled. We are all the poorer for it and the Antitrust Laws are a large part of the failure of the Twentieth Century "COMMONS" to equal Mr. Rockefeller's achievement.

162

The Antitrust Laws give the "WANNABE PEERS" a powerful tool to retard and even reverse the growth of the economy, thus increasing the misery and the ranks of their primary constituency, the poor.

CHAPTER EIGHT

THE BUREAUCRACY-ICC

One could argue that the establishment of bureaucracies was the "WANNABE PEERS" first big victory because the first bureaucracy, the INTERSTATE COMMERCE COMMISSION[48] (ICC) was established by the passage of the Interstate Commerce Act of 1887, three years before the passage of the Sherman Antitrust Act. However, the ICC Commission had a very limited scope. Originally, it only had power to set maximum shipping rates, whereas the Sherman Antitrust Act affected the whole economy.

The establishment of the ICC created these two new terms in political science:

* "IRON TRIANGLE[50] (see fig. 8) is a description of how the "SPECIAL INTEREST GROUPS", the Congress (many members are "WANNABE PEERS" acting in their own interest) and the bureaucrats act in collusion to exploit the "COMMONS" and "PAWNS". The "WANNABE PEERS" objective is to use government force to control the "COMMONS" and reward the "PAWNS" for political support. The bureaucracy is the perfect vehicle to accomplish that. Congress wants to be reelected and increase their individual power and the bureaucracy wants to expand its power and increase its

164

budget. The "IRON TRIANGLE" is the ordinary operation of bureaucracy. It is not unusual for the "WANNABE PEERS" and the "PAWNS" to trade places as the political advantage shifts. The bureaucrat's only allegiance is to political power.

- "REGULATORY CAPTURE"[53] describes the condition that occurs when the bureaucracy matures; the infighting ends and the "WANNABE PEERS" achieve control of the regulatory process. They then reap the rewards of the use of government force against competitors and customers ("COMMONS" or "PAWNS"). The "PAWNS" (often the consumer) support the creation of the agency in expectation of obtaining favorable treatment from the bureaucrats, ignoring the historical evidence that the "WANNABE PEERS" would seize control of the regulatory agency and exploit the "PAWNS".

The "PAWNS" and "WANNABE PEERS" often speak of the evils of the "REGULATORY CAPTURE" and the "IRON TRIANGLE". Yet, the evil of the regulations is not determined by who is receiving the "SPECIAL FAVORS" or who is being exploited. The evil is the fact that it is the agency, not the "FREE MARKET FORCES" that controls the economy. When the "FREE MARKET FORCES" are perverted we all lose, except those who are the recipient of the "SPECIAL FAVORS" and many times the recipient enjoys only a fleeting advantage. History is full of "WANNABE PEERS" supporting the creation of a bureaucracy and gaining special favors until other "WANNABE PEERS" obtain greater political power and reverses the direction of the "special favors", often with disastrous results for those instrumental in the creation of the bureaucracy. Talk about poetic justice.

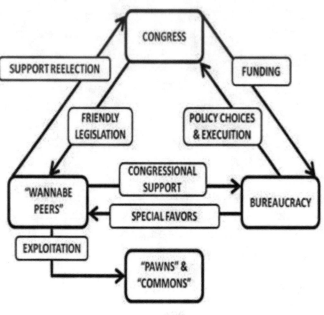

THE IRON TRIANGLE - THE POLITICS OF COLLUSION

FIG. 8

Unfortunately, the concept of the bureaucracy would be expanded. The power of the government agencies would be expanded to control whole sections of the economy with the power to act as legislator, police, prosecutor, judge and jury. These agencies:

- CREATE RULES AND REGULATIONS (THE LEGISLATIVE FUNCTION)

- INVESTIGATE THE "COMMONS" FOR COMPLIANCE WITH THEIR RULES WITHOUT WARRANTS. (THE POLICE FUNCTION AND JUDGE FUNCTION)
- CITE THE "COMMONS" FOR VIOLATIONS OF THEIR RULES. (THE PROSECUTOR FUNCTION)
- PUNISH THE "COMMONS" FOR VIOLATING THE RULES THAT THE AGENCY CREATED. (THE JUDGE and JURY FUNCTION}

Bureaucracies are an important part of the "WANNABEE PEERS'" plan to create the economic crisis that can be used to eradicate the last vestiges of Capitalism (individual freedom). Since the bureaucrats make the rules and regulations, they provide perfect cover for the "WANNABE PEERS". If the detrimental effects of the bureaucrats' actions become general knowledge, the "WANNABE PEERS" can blame the faceless bureaucrat and promise to correct the problem by "reining in the out of control bureaucracy". Instead of being blamed, the "WANNABE PEERS" in Congress spin the problems caused by the bureaucrat's actions to gain political advantage. Many accept the spin and ignore the obvious fact that the bureaucracy was created and controlled by the "WANNABE PEERS" in Congress.

By definition, the bureaucratic rules and regulations inhibit or prohibit the creation of wealth. If the bureaucratic rules and regulations were in the best interest of the "COMMONS", the "technology dividend" compliance would be assured by the forces of the free market and the agency would be irrelevant. The inevitable effect of bureaucratic rules and regulations is to impede economic progress, by maintaining the "status quo", increasing production cost and

167

enforcing a pressure group's agenda. In summary, the bureaucracy is a blatant attack on the "technology dividend" that impedes economic growth and prevents or limits any increase in the standard of living. Continued growth in the bureaucracy can only result in increased poverty. Of course, the net effect of increased poverty will be an increase in the "WANNABE PEERS" constituency.

The government cannot force freedom; it can only promote freedom by protecting the individual from the initiation of physical force. Often, the "PAWNS" who demand that the bureaucracy use force to give them an advantage over the "COMMONS", find that they lose much more than they gain.

Government agencies exhibit the following characteristics:

- The primary purpose of any bureaucracy is to increase its budget. The bureaucracy's eternal quest is to increase its power to justify an increase in its budget. An increase in the budget means more employees and that means promotions. The increasing of the bureaucrat's budget is equivalent to profit in the "private sector" that allows the company to grow.

- The desire for a larger budget will cause the bureaucracy to attempt to increase its power by expanding the rules and regulations. The bureaucracy power increases come at the expense of individual freedom. The economic damage resulting from this loss of individual freedom compounds with these constant increases in power. The result is growth of the "WANNABE PEERS" core constituency, the poor.

168

- The actions of the bureaucrats, despite the claims to the contrary, are manipulated by the "WANNABE PEERS" (the Congress and political appointees).
- The "WANNABE PEERS" control the bureaucrat's budget.
- The actions of any government agency are controlled by the "WANNABE PEERS" in cooperation with the leaders of the affected industry. Care is always taken to disguise the influence. Was this fact lost on the "WANNABE PEERS" when the first agency was established? Hardly! In 1889, William H. H. Miller[48], US Attorney General, said

"**The Commission is, or can be made, of great use to the railroads. It satisfies the popular clamor for a government supervision of the railroads, while at the same time that supervision is almost entirely nominal.**"

Mr. Miller was describing the first US regulatory agency, the Interstate Commerce Commission. Need more proof that the "WANNABE PEERS" knew that the agencies do not act in the public interest? Evaluating the actions of government agencies in 1913, President Woodrow Wilson[52][48] wrote:

"**If the government is to tell big business men how to run their business, then don't you see that big business men have to get closer to the government even than they are now? Don't you see that they must capture the government, in order not to be restrained too much by it? Must capture the government? They have already captured it.**"

These two quotes should erase any doubts that those who were instrumental in afflicting us with these government agencies knew that the agencies were a threat to individual freedom and would try to maintain the "status quo".

The enforcement powers[35], [36], [37] of the bureaucrats provide the "WANNABE PEERS" a means of controlling the "COMMONS", forcing them to support the "WANNABE PEERS'" agenda.

The loss of individual freedom, caused by increasing power of the bureaucrats, either inhibits or prohibits the creation of wealth. Can you imagine a bureaucrat mandating that Thomas Edison develop and produce the light bulb? However, it is easy to imagine a bureaucrat establishing rules and regulations to inhibit the use of the light bulb with the purpose of maintaining the market for kerosene (the primary source of home lighting before the light bulb). The quality and cost of the light produced by electricity could not be matched by kerosene. It was a clear case of the blatant use of a technological advantage by a predatory "COMMON" to destroy the technologically challenged competitor.

Do inequities exist in a free market? Certainly! Innovation brings problems as well as prosperity. These problems can be solved by "trial and error" in the free market. These inequities cannot be solved by the use of force, especially when the objective of the use of force is political advantage[50], [53].

The "preponderance of propaganda" portrays the bureaucrats as experts in their field whose objective is the welfare of the public. That their primary objective is to

170

increase their budget is a conflict of interest is not even considered.

The creation of the bureaucracy was certainly a win-win situation for the "WANNABE PEERS". The bureaucracy is a cancer that feeds on its own growth, as it destroys individual freedom and wealth (the recipe for growth of the "WANNABE PEERS" constituency). All that is needed to assure the bureaucracies' growth is to approve the ever expanding budget requests.

BIRTH OF BUREAUCRACY—THE INTERSTATE COMMERCE COMMISSION[48] (ICC):

How are bureaucracies created? A new bureaucracy is created by act of Congress whenever a group of "WANNABE PEERS" achieves the influence to cause Congress to act on its behalf. Are the bureaucracies as evil and destructive as this book would have you believe? Reviewing the history of the first (the ICC) of these government agencies, the Interstate Commerce Commission (ICC) will allow the reader to make that decision.

To analyze and expose the damage done by all the alphabetical monstrosities created since invention of the bureaucrat would be both time consuming and counter-productive, so the detailed analysis will only cover the first fifty years of the operation of the first bureaucracy, the Interstate Commerce Commission (ICC).

The ICC was created by act of Congress in 1887 and passed into history in 1995. The ICC can be evaluated free of the emotion that might affect the evaluation of more recent bureaucratic adventures. Ample information is available to fully evaluate the creation, operation and results of the ICC's first fifty

171

years and the ICC's first fifty years is fully representative of the operation and the evil of the bureaucracy.

The railroad industry was by far the largest industry in the United States at the time the ICC was created. The large railroads had both branch and trunk lines. Where two railroads had trunk lines between cities, competition caused the freight rates to vacillate between "cutthroat competition" and rates set by agreements between the two parties. Because the agreements lacked an enforcement mechanism, the agreement to control the freight rates was ineffective. The use of force is necessary to maintain a monopoly. The result was chaotic rate changes on the trunk lines. On the branch lines, many controlled by small railroads, there was no competition and rates were higher than those on the trunk lines. The high rates on the branch lines were resented by the customers.

The Granger movement, once a social and educational rural farm organization, started a lobbying effort to represent farmers in their conflict with the railroads. The Grange was successful in having states enact laws to control freight rates but the state laws were not effective because of limited powers and legal challenges by the railroads. So the fight moved to the Congress. The Grange considered the rates on the branch lines to be price gouging and wanted the government to force the rates lower. In the words of a Vice President of the Pennsylvania Railroad:

"a large majority of the railroads in the United States would be delighted if a railroad commission could make rates upon their traffic which would assure them of six percent

dividends, and I have no doubt, with such a guarantee, they would be glad to come under the direct supervision and operation of the national government".

Taken at face value, what this means is that the railroads would surrender their freedom for security and a guaranteed profit. They wanted a government coerced cartel. Well, the railroads achieved their objective and the results validated Mr. Franklin's[19] statement that those who would trade freedom for security deserve neither.

In summary, the railroads wanted government enforced cartel which guaranteed them a profit, the Grange and other shippers wanted low and consistent rates and the Congress just wanted to be reelected.

The conflict resulted in creation of the Interstate Commerce Commission. The law creating the ICC required that all railroad charges be reasonable and just, whatever that meant. The original ICC had to use the courts to enforce its orders and railroads were able to circumvent the rules when it was advantageous. The customers thought they were getting rates that were reasonable and just, the railroads had established a mechanism for a cartel to enforce the rate agreements and the Congress could claim to have helped the "little guy". The only source of the expertise to set rates was the railroads. The railroads had the money to influence the Congress. Within ten years, with the combination of technical expertise and financial resources, the railroads effectively took control of the agency. The "REGULATORY CAPTURE" was complete. The railroads had won the battle, but not the war. "REGULATORY

CAPTURE" made the railroads very profitable for years but "SPECIAL INTEREST", not even thought of in 1887, would use the ICC against the railroads and destroys the railroad's dominance of transportation industry.

The "GOLDEN AGE OF THE RAILROAD" ended shortly after the turn of the Century and the railroad's status as a "WANNABE PEER" began to change to that of "PAWN". President Theodore Roosevelt effectively ended the domination of the ICC by the railroads with the passage of the Elkins Act of 1903 and the Hepburn Act of 1906. The Elkins Act ended the practice of railroads giving rebates to valued customers and required the publishing of the freight rates. The Elkins Act gave the ICC the right to establish maximum rates, control terminals, pipelines and other facilities under ICC jurisdiction. The most important change was to place the burden of proof on the carrier and shipper instead of the ICC in appeals.

Railroads were in favor of ending the rebates but not the strict rate control. The law added to the ICC's power and required that the rates be published. The volume of freight, committing to future shipping schedules and other actions (the economy of scale) by the large volume shippers that made their freight more profitable to the railroads than smaller shippers, a free market would recognize the advantages and reward the volume shipper with lower rates. Because the high volume business was more profitable, the railroads made concessions to obtain that business. The ICC saw these rates as discriminatory to the small shipper and the setting of the rates by the ICC removed the advantage of lower rates from the volume shippers and also removed the incentive for the volume shippers to cooperate with the railroads to reduce the railroad's cost. The increased cost to the volume shipper was most likely passed on to the consumer. Any incentive for innovation by the railroads and their customers had been destroyed.

It is impossible to estimate the cost of this lack of innovation to the economy over the next 100 years. However, when the railroad industry was deregulated in 1980, the railroad freight rates[48] dropped by 54% in 27 years and the profitability of railroads improved.

When the economy is controlled by "WANNABE PEERS" instead of market forces, everybody loses. The law increased the marginal producer's ability to compete, reduced the volume shippers' "economy of scale" and destroyed any incentive for innovation in the operating of the railroads. The consumer did not even recognize the source of the increased cost. The "WANNABE PEERS" had maintained the "status quo" and struck another blow against the "technology dividend". When coercion replaces innovation, we all lose in the long run, even those who are afforded the temporary benefit that accrues to the "WANNABE PEERS" from government coercion against their competitors.

In the late 1800's the railroads, assured of profits and relieved of the necessity of innovation, settled into a period of stagnation. A once proud growing and aggressive industry had been completely neutered by government intervention. The railroads days as "WANNABE PEERS" were over. They had been reduced to the level of "PAWNS" and the industry would suffer until the partial deregulation of the 1980's.

The United States entered WWI in 1917, and the railroads having lived a somewhat effortless existence under the shelter of the government's benevolent coercion for years, were unable to respond to the requirements of a war time economy. To obtain the transportation required to execute the war effort, the government seized the railroads and operated them until March 1, 1920.

When the railroads were returned to their owners, the regulatory objectives had changed considerably by the "Transportation Act of 1920. The law expanded the rate making powers of the ICC. The Act directed the ICC to set rates to provide a fair return on the entire railroad investment and confiscate earnings exceeding a prescribed rate (labeled recaptured earnings). Any incentive for innovation that remained was totally destroyed by the new rules. The railroads entered a new period of stagnation.

The ICC encouraged the merging of the railroads with the expectation of strengthening the industry. The Act charged the ICC with creating a "National Consolidation Plan" for the railroads. The plan was never implemented and the requirement for the plan was rescinded in 1933. The damage caused to the railroads by the uncertainty created by the "National Consolidation Plan" requirement is anybody's guess, but it certainly did not help the railroads. The railroads were profitable during the "Roaring Twenties". However, the brief prosperity did not offset the weak credit structures caused by the government operation during the war years and the years of enforced competition (prohibiting the merging of railroads that served the same market). Preventing the merging required the railroads to maintain duplicate facilities and had made the railroads vulnerable to an economic turndown.

Adding to the problem caused by the weak credit structure was the new competition in the transportation industry. Automobiles, airplanes, water carriers and trucks now competed with the railroads for the transportation dollar. The close regulation of the railroads by the ICC made timely changes to rates and services impossible. The delays caused by waiting for regulatory approval prevented the railroads from being competitive with other forms of transportation. The motor carriers became the new "WANNABE PEERS" of the transportation industry and benefited from the "handcuffs" the ICC applied to the railroads. The ICC's manipulation of the transportation industry created the "long haul" trucking industry. Promotion of the "long haul" trucking industry caused huge misapplication of capital and higher overall freight rates. The Teamsters Union became the "WANNABE PEERS" and the railroad's status as "PAWNS" was complete.

The financial depression of the 1930's forced many railroads into receivership. Something had to be done to avoid the total collapse of the railroad industry.

Somehow, it never occurred to those in power that the problem could be solved simply by eliminating the ICC and letting the free market produce the solution.

CHAPTER EIGHT

In 1933, the rules to be used in setting rates were changed, requiring the ICC to use more of the analysis that a competent railroad executive would use to set rates. The profit limit (recaptured earnings) was eliminated as was the requirement to create a "National Consolidation Plan". Elimination of the "recaptured earnings" regulation had little immediate effect because there was little profit available. The other unregulated carriers still enjoyed a significant advantage over the railroads. The **"JOYOUS AND RUDDY**[41]**"** motor carriers exploited the railroads' regulatory servitude to build an industry that could never have existed with an unfettered railroad industry. We all paid higher freight rates and huge investments were made in equipment to create a higher cost, "technologically challenged" industry.

The Congress, having learned nothing from the economic disasters caused by the ICC, passed the Motor Carrier Act of 1935 which made Motor Carriers subject to ICC regulations. In 1940 the Transportation Act of 1940 added the Water Carriers. The political clout of the Motor Carriers and Water Carriers was able to exclude both large and important areas of their business from ICC interference. The Motor Carriers continued to enjoy their status as "WANNABE PEERS" in the "IRON TRIANGLE" (see fig. 8).

The Congress passed a "Declaration of National Transportation Policy" declaring that the "Interstate Commerce Act" be administered so as to preserve the inherent advantages of each mode of transportation. Hey, isn't that what the free market does?

The saga of the ICC had a somewhat happy ending. By the 1970's the regulatory handcuffs had the railroad industry in shambles. Bankruptcies were common and revenue failed to cover the cost of maintenance. Service levels were still deteriorating and rates were rising. Just before the complete collapse of the industry, Congress passed the Staggers Act which significantly, reduced but did not completely eliminate the railroad's regulatory burden. However, the Act was adequate to save the railroad industry[56]. Rates, productivity and volume had been dormant for over 15 years by 1980. Between 1980 and 2007, productivity of the railroad industry increased by almost a factor of 3[56]. Volume doubled and rates dropped (adjusted for inflation) to half the rates at the time the Staggers Act was passed. The railroad industry, free of some of the regulatory burden, was making a comeback. The Railroad Industry was removed from the endangered species list. Today, freight rates in the United States are the lowest in the world. One wonders what could have been accomplished if the industry were completely deregulated or if the ICC had never existed.

The purpose of evaluating the performance of the ICC is to show how government intervention in the economy destroys prosperity. Evaluating 54 years of the operation of the agency and the rebound of the Railroad Industry, after even partial deregulation adequately proves the fallacy of the bureaucracy. The point is made but the fiasco of the ICC continued on until 1995 when many of its powers were transferred to other agencies.

Perhaps the progress made by the Railroad Industry since the deregulation is a better measure of bureaucracies' capacity to destroy the economy than analysis of the damage to the economy done by the ICC's regulations.

The ICC did irreparable harm to both the transportation industry and the economy. It is impossible to determine either the cost of this bungling to the economy or the productivity losses due to the stifling of innovation by the regulatory burden.

SUMMARY – BUREAUCRATIC EFFECTS ON THE ECONOMY:

Inequities occur in the free market, but left to its own devices, the free market will correct itself. The bureaucracy will only perpetuate itself.

The analysis of the ICC's performance demonstrated that the purpose of a bureaucracy is to reward the "WANNABE PEERS", placate the "PAWNS", increase the budget of the bureaucracy and reelect the Congress. The analysis of the performance of the ICC is offered as an example of the normal operation of a bureaucracy. It validates the theories of the "IRON TRIANGLE"[50] and "REGULATORY CAPTURE"[53].

Most of the problems in the United States today can be traced to bureaucratic meddling in the economy. The bureaucratic bungling has either created or contributed to the following:

- High cost of health care
- High employment cost
- Dependence on foreign energy
- Deterioration of public education
- Deterioration of the railroad industry

- Extended the life span and the agony of many marginal producers
- Suppressed innovation
- Perpetuated poverty with self serving administration of the welfare effort
- Added to the reelection of many "WANNABE PEERS" and their quest for ever increasing power
- Provided a weapon to the "WANNABE PEERS" to silence and control opposition to their quest for power

Many man-years of research and reams of paper would be required to detail all the damage that the bureaucracy has done to the economy and individual liberty. Detailing the threats and intimidation to the "COMMONS" on behalf of the "WANNABE PEERS" could consume several lifetimes. This analysis of the ICC's performance and a little imagination provides all the proof of the evils perpetuated by a faceless bureaucracy that any rational person could require.

Is there any doubt that the purpose of the bureaucracy is to increase the power of the "WANNABE PEERS"? Correcting the inequities of the free market is not the purpose of the bureaucracy; it is just fodder for the "preponderance of propaganda".

CHAPTER NINE

INFLATION AND MANIPULATION OF THE DOLLAR:

A good definition of inflation[62] is "**a general and progressive increase in prices; in inflation everything gets more valuable except money**".

Over the long run, the value of the dollar (see fig.4) is equal to the nation's wealth divided by the money/credit supply (number of dollars and available credit). Although many things can cause short term divergence from this formula, eventually the piper must be paid and expanding the money/credit supply will reduce the purchasing power of the dollar. Of course, reducing money/credit supply increases the value of the dollar.

Increasing the cost of real assets also reduces the value of the dollar. The government's meddling in the economy by restricting the availability of "consumable assets", increasing the cost of production, restricting the use of "active assets" (means of production), inhibiting or preventing innovation, increasing the cost of harvesting natural resources and preventing the harvesting of natural resources reduces the value of the dollar. Consumption of assets reduces the value of the dollar as the assets are no longer part of the nation's wealth.

When projects or businesses fail to produce value in excess of the investment, the wealth is destroyed instead of being created.

When government regulations cause increased prices to the consumer, those increased prices are blamed on the "COMMONS" (producer). The "WANNABE PEERS'" propaganda campaign against their chosen "enemy", the "RICH", often successfully blames the "COMMONS" for the results of bureaucratic meddling. Many times the bureaucratic enforced regulations reward the "WANNABE PEERS'" supporters ("PAWNS") and exploit the "COMMONS" (producers) while depleting the value of the dollar.

The supply of money and credit is controlled by the Federal Reserve.

Innovation, allowed by individual freedom, increases the nation's wealth and the value of the dollar. Innovation increases individual productivity, the source of the "technology dividend". Bureaucratic regulations and laws, protecting the marginal producer or restricting harvesting of natural resources, increase production cost and deplete the nation's wealth. Bureaucratic rules and laws reducing individual freedom limit innovation. Bureaucracies and legislators can only implement their initiatives by use of force. If their initiatives were in the best interest of the economy (and you), the free market would cause them to be implemented and the use of force would be irrelevant. Therefore, the action of the government is at best neutral and can only reduce the nation's wealth and the value of the dollar.

Taxes remove money and credit from the economy; government expenditures consume assets or invest assets in projects such as infrastructure. The consumed assets are removed from the nation's wealth. The investments, when successful, add to the nation's wealth. When taxes and government expenditures that consume wealth are equal (a rare occurrence) the value of the dollar is unaffected.

THE BIG LIE:
The "WANNABE PEERS" would have you believe that tax increases only occur when the legislature enacts or increases a tax. **Not so!** The tax is levied when the government spends the money. Enacting tax only affects how the tax is paid and who pays it. If taxes don't cover expenditures, inflation results, and everyone who has money pays the tax with the loss of purchasing power. If money/credit is created to buy the assets, the money/credit supply is increased and the nation's wealth is reduced by consuming the assets. The economy is a complex device and the effect of government spending and tax receipts can take years to be reflected in the value of the dollar. This is especially true when the act is complicated by government borrowing to delay the inflationary effect or significant innovation creates new wealth. With the level of bureaucratic intervention in the economy, the creation of new innovation is highly restricted. Eventually, the loan must be repaid. Since the government rarely has a surplus of tax money over expenses, the only reasonable outcome is increasing the money/credit supply. The government cannot

spend money without either using money accumulated by taxes or creating inflation. Inflation is simply "STEALTH TAXATION".

Manipulation of the medium of exchange, "money", wasn't new to the United States. Over the life of the Roman Empire, the content of the coins[22] changed from almost pure silver to almost pure copper. The Romans just melted the coins, threw more copper in the pot and struck coins from the diluted metal. However, the invention of paper money and bank credit has simplified the manipulation of the money/credit supply for the modern "WANNABE PEERS". Even printing money is no longer necessary; the Federal Reserve can expand the money/credit supply with a computer entry.

Control of the money supply by the "WANNABE PEERS" requires a government controlled central bank. There were two (2) unsuccessful attempts to establish a central banking system. Both attempts resulted in a central banking system that lasted 20 years; the last ended in 1836. From 1836 to 1865 banking was handled by state chartered banks and uncharted "free banks" who issued bank notes redeemable in gold. The National Banking Act of 1863 established nationally chartered banks. These banks created paper money backed by U.S. Government securities instead of gold. This was an early attempt of the "WANNABE PEERS" to divorce the dollar from hard currency. The primary purpose of the paper money was to finance the Civil War. The paper money created during this period was called "GREENBACKS"[60]. Even though the "WANNABE PEERS" did not control the banks, banks were able to expand the money/credit supply by manipulating deposits and creating

185

credit in excess of the deposits. Economic booms and busts resulted from excessive creation of credit and losses due to inept and sometimes criminal use of that credit. However, the requirement for the banks to pay depositors in gold on demand restrained the banks from unlimited increases in credit.

The third attempt to create a national bank was successful and the Federal Reserve opened for business on November 16, 1914; just in time to use inflating the money/credit supply to finance World War I.

The United States did not enter the "GREAT WAR" until April 6, 1917 but the War in Europe started in 1914. The Federal Reserve, using "BANKER'S ACCEPTANCES" (instruments of credit for the "ALLIED POWERS"). Indirectly helped the "ALLIED POWERS" finance their war effort until the United States entered the war in 1917. World War I ended with the Armistice on November 11, 1918. The increase in money supply and the production of implements of war resulted in an inflation rate of 7.64% in 1916 and the inflation rate was above 15% through 1920. Inflating the money supply during the war destroyed much of the value of the dollar and a short depression followed the war. The inflation rate was -10.85% in 1921 and -6.1% in 1922. The manipulation of the money supply to end the inflation created a minor economic crisis. The purpose of the Federal Reserve Board was to end the boom and bust economy that had plagued the country for the past hundred years. It failed in 1920 and the results since 1920 have not been any better. The Federal Reserve could increase the money/credit supply at will but money was backed by gold which placed some limits, at least theoretically. That ended in the mid 1930's when the "WANNABE PEERS" succeeded in taking the country off the gold standard.

INFLATION IN THE TWENTIETH CENTURY:
Calculation of the rate of inflation is a complicated and imprecise science. Goods and services that are commonplace today were not available at any price 100 years ago. Innovation creates new or replacement products and services with increased capability so that a simple change in price does not always adequately describe the change in value.

A "GOOGLE search" for an inflation calculator[55] results in over 20 pages of listings. Only 4 versions will be considered here. Since the "WANNABE PEERS'" first successes were in the late Nineteenth Century and took effect in the early Twentieth Century the rate of inflation from 1900 to 2007 was analyzed and compared to the inflation rate that occurred during the Nineteenth Century. The results from the four calculators[55] are:

- Westegg.com calculates that $1 in 1900 dollar is equal to $24.61 in 2007.
- Tom's inflation calculator http://www.halfhill.com/inflation.html sets the inflation rate from 1900 to 2007 at $27.71 and wage inflation from 1914 to 2007 at $19.73
- Moneychmp.com http://www.moneychimp.com/articles/econ/inflation calculator.htm calculates that the annualized inflation rate was 3.1 percent. $1.00 in 1900 had the same purchasing power as $26.58 in 2007.

- The United States Department of Labor web site http://www.bls.gov/data/inflation calculato r.htm calculates that $1.00 in 1913 has the same purchasing power as $20.94 in 2007. (1913 was the earliest date available on this website).

The four calculators yield fairly close answers and agree that the inflation rate of our currency was quite significant over the 107 years. These calculators seem to agree that the dollar was worth about twenty-five times as much in 1900 as it was worth in 2008. This compares to an inflation rate just over 10 percent for the entire Nineteenth Century.

Commodity prices are another way to check the inflation calculators. Gold[58] is often considered a standard of value and an ounce of gold sold for $20.67 in 1900. In 2007 that same ounce of gold sold for $845.40, almost 41 times what it sold for at the turn of the Century. Speculation (the price of an ounce of gold varied from $1032.70 to $880.30 in 2008) and legislation sometimes affects the price of gold so the price of gold is not a completely valid measure of inflation.

Silver[59] sold for $0.648 an ounce in 1900 and closed at $14.76 at the end of 2007. The price of silver at the end of 2007 was almost 23 times its price in 1900. Both speculation and industrial activity affect the price of silver at a given date. Depletion of easily harvested ore, technological advances in mining and processing of ore affects the price of metals as does changes in demand for industrial uses. These factors prevent any metal or other commodity from being a totally reliable measure of inflation; however, the price of gold and silver tend to confirm the "inflation calculators".

Any way you look at it, the value of the dollar in 1900 was about 25 times its value in 2008. The rate of inflation varies widely and with large increases when factors such as war increases government expenditures and reduces the availability of commodities and production facilities to use for producing "consumable assets". During the period 1914 to 1925 (WW I), the inflation rate per year varied from a negative 10.85% in 1921 to a positive 17.80% in 1917. Short periods of high inflation are usually followed by periods of deflation that tend to reduce the overall effect of inflation over time. The following inflation rates were calculated using "Tom's Inflation Calculator" on the website http://www.halfhill.com/inflation.html. Between 1900 and 1940 the inflation rate 1.91 to 1; from 1940 to 2000 the inflation rate was almost 12 to 1. From 2000 to 2008 the inflation rate was 1.24 to 1. During that period the purchasing power of the dollar declined from $1.00 to $0.806. It appears that the average inflation rate is increasing with time and the power of the "WANNABE PEERS". For those who wonder why the inflation rates from 1900-1940, 1940-2000 and 2000-2008 don't add up to 25, it is because the rates compound.

Inflation is very real and the goods and services the government accrues by inflating the money/credit supply is a significant portion of the economy. However, the portion of goods and services paid for by inflating the money supply is even greater than the inflation rate would indicate. The

189

"technology dividend", the increase in productivity produced by innovation, grew by a factor of 7.77 to 1 during the Twentieth Century. This estimate of growth of the "technology dividend" is based upon the increase in the "real gross domestic product per capita" (individual productivity, adjusted for inflation) between 1900 and 2008. Had the money/credit supply not been inflated, the technology dividend would have increased the value of the dollar by a factor of 7.77 to 1 (a dollar in 2008 would have had the purchasing power of 7.77 1900 dollars). Instead of losing value, the dollar would have gained value.

If the deflating effect of the "technology dividend" is added to the calculated inflation rate, the real effect of inflating the money/credit supply was 32 to 1. Without the "technology dividend" the purchasing power of the 2008 dollar would have been about three cents ($0.03) in 1900 dollars.

Based upon "Tom's Inflation Calculator" the inflation rate from 1800 to 1900 was only 1.12 to 1. From 1900 to 2007 it was 25 to 1. In other words, in 1900 the dollar had the purchasing power of slightly over eighty-nine cents in 1800 dollars and in 2007 the dollar only had the purchasing power of 0.04 cents in 1900 dollars.

Why was there little to no change in the inflation rate during the 1800s yet during the 1900's it was over 25 to 1? Three factors are primarily responsible:

The "WANNABE PEER'S" first victories over individual freedom took effect at the turn of the Century (1900). New initiatives by the

"WANNABE PEERS" added to the earlier victories and the effects compounded throughout the Twentieth Century. Each of these victories increased government control over the individual. Of course, the results of more government control increased the cost of production and limited innovation.

- The nation's wealth was reduced and inflation was the result.
- The creation of the Federal Reserve early in the century simplified the manipulation of the money/credit supply and gave complete control of the money/credit supply to the "WANNABE PEERS".
- In the mid-1930s, the "WANNABE PEERS" took the nation off the gold standard. Elimination of the gold standard removed any constraints on the printing of money or creation of credit.

There's no doubt that the rate of inflation increased with the loss of individual freedom and the seizure of the control of the money/credit supply by the "WANNABE PEERS".

EFFECTS OF INFLATION:

- Inflation is "STEALTH TAXATION" that gives the "WANNABE PEERS" control of goods and services without the "COMMONS" or "PAWNS" even realizing their wealth has been confiscated.
- With a progressive income tax rate, inflation simply increases the effective tax rate without any action from the "WANNABE PEERS".

- Replacement of inventory and obsolete or worn out equipment must be made at a higher cost than the original investment, requiring that additional capital be deployed just to stay even.
- Irresponsible expansion of the money/credit supply leads to boom and bust economy, providing the "WANNABE PEERS" with a series of economic crises. Each economic crisis provides the "WANNABE PEERS" the opportunity to increase their power over the individual.
- Penalizes all creditors. Debt is repaid to creditors with dollars that have lost part of their purchasing power.
- Anticipation of inflation increases the interest rate demanded by creditors.
- Inflation prevents citizens from providing for emergencies and old age, increasing the proportion of the population in poverty, another factor to increase the "WANNABE PEERS" constituency.
- Highly regulated industries, exploited by bureaucratic meddling, are prevented from changing prices to compensate for inflation. This prevents the generation of revenue required to maintain and expand services. Eventually the shortfall in revenue creates a crisis allowing the "WANNABE PEERS" to blame the "COMMONS" and usurp more power.
- The inflation rate is not constant. The variation makes it impossible to include the effects in long term planning.
- Inflation makes it difficult, if not impossible, to store value. Storing value is one of the reasons for money.

SUMMARY:

Even an omnipotent President and congressional majority cannot violate the "FIRST LAW OF THERMODYNAMICS". As applied to economics, the "FIRST LAW OF THERMODYNAMICS" means that you can't get something for nothing and that wealth must be created before it can be consumed. Regulations and laws will not create wealth. Regulations and laws can only inhibit creation of wealth or redistribute wealth. Increasing the money/credit supply does not increase the amount of goods and services (the nation's wealth) but it can change who controls the wealth. It allows the "WANNABE PEERS" to confiscate the "COMMONS'" (producer) wealth and redistribute the wealth to the "PAWNS" in exchange for political support.

When the "WANNABE PEERS" have the power to seize the "COMMONS" wealth, there is no incentive for the "COMMONS" to produce wealth!

CHAPTER TEN

EARMARKS

Exactly what is an "EARMARK"[54]? Wikipedia, the free encyclopedia[1] lists the following definition of "EARMARKS": **"In US politics, an "EARMARK" is a congressional provision that directs approved funds to be spent on specific projects or that directs specific exemptions from taxes or mandated fees"**.

A simpler, more direct definition would be **"a law conferring special privileges or distributing wealth to political cronies"**. If you accept this definition, unless you were the recipient of the favor why would you ever reelect a Congressperson who sponsored an "EARMARK"?

The creation of a new enterprise or project requires capital. If the project is successful, wealth is created. If the project fails, the capital invested in the project is lost. Capitalism requires that the entrepreneur obtain the capital (wealth) to finance a new project. If previous successes have allowed the entrepreneur to create enough wealth, the entrepreneur can finance the project. If the project requires more capital than the entrepreneur possesses, the additional capital must be obtained from

194

investors. To obtain the capital, the entrepreneur must convince investors that the project will create wealth and provide them with a profit. Before they will invest in the project the investors must be convinced both of the personal integrity of the entrepreneur and the validity of the plan that he proposes.

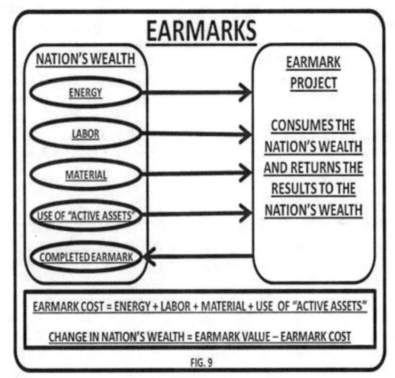

FIG. 9

To obtain an "EARMARK", the "WANNABE PEER" must convince the Congressperson that providing him with the "EARMARK" will be to his political advantage. There is no other consideration. The creation of wealth or profit is not an issue, only political advantage is considered. The real entrepreneur would never request an "EARMARK", because to accept money from the government is to accept a partner who is interested in political gain, not creating wealth or profit. This type of partner would prevent the entrepreneur from competing effectively in the marketplace.

Decisions based on political expediency instead of profit potential will only result in the destruction of wealth. **Capitalism is the most efficient method of deploying capital that mankind has yet invented.**

The "WANNABE PEERS" use their "preponderance of propaganda" to denounce "EARMARKS" **even as they enact new "EARMARKS".**

Even with the best of preparation and maximum effort, many projects fail and the investment and all the effort expended is lost. However, some succeed and produce tremendous wealth. Some examples are FORD MOTOR COMPANY, STANDARD OIL, APPLE, GOOGLE, MICROSOFT and IBM but the list is endless.

To fund a project with an "EARMARK" it is only necessary to convince the Congressperson that it will contribute to reelection.

Have "EARMARKS" ever created even a fraction of the wealth produced by a successful private enterprise? Few "EARMARKS" expend less wealth than was used to start the **FORD MOTOR COMPANY or APPLE COMPUTER** or the other private enterprise projects that have produced great wealth. The use of political expediency instead of profit potential to select which projects to fund is a prescription for economic disaster.

Can you imagine an "EARMARK" funding Thomas Edison and directing him to develop the light bulb? If an "EARMARK" had been passed to fund Thomas Edison's invention of the light bulb, do you think he would have accepted the money along with a partner whose objective was political power instead of profit? Hardly! If he had, we would probably still be using candles or kerosene lamps.

To be fair, there have been a few examples where government initiated investment created great wealth, but you can count them on the fingers of one hand. Remember the Erie Canal and the G.I. Bill (for veterans of WW II)? However, these programs could not be classed as "EARMARKS".

It is interesting to note that neither of these programs was initiated to benefit a small group of "PAWNS" at the expense of all the citizens. There have been many government programs that consumed great wealth or redistributed wealth from the "COMMONS" (producer) to the "PEERS'" political cronies.

In practice, few "EARMARKS" return any value to the Nation's Wealth. Some even return a liability, reducing the Nation's Wealth even more than the original cost. Allowing members of Congress to place an "EARMARK" has been used to bribe them to vote for bills they would otherwise oppose. It would be impossible to list all the damage done to our individual freedom and the economy by ""EARMARKS"".

In 2008(the latest year that data is available) the appropriations for "EARMARKS" totaled $16.5 billion spent on 11,524 "EARMARKS". The UNITED STATES' "Nominal GDP[5]" for 2008 was $14,264.6 billion. So why should we concern ourselves over such a paltry sum of $16.5 billion? After all, it is less than 0.12% of the GDP. The "real GDP per capita[5]" average growth over the last fifty years has been 2.13% per year. This is probably the best available measurement of the increase in individual productivity. So the "EARMARKS" consume well over 5% of the yearly growth in productivity.

$16.5 billion could provide the seed money for hundreds of new enterprises with the capacity to create unlimited wealth.

The nation's assets (Energy, labor, active assets (production capacity) and materials) are limited. Once those assets are consumed they are no longer available for productive use. Most of these assets are used to produce "consumable assets" so the amount of assets available for economic growth is extremely limited. Any waste of this available capital has a significant effect on future economic growth and your prosperity.

More important than the dollar waste are the types of assets squandered. Many of the "EARMARKS" are grants for scientific research, paying for the waste of scientific talent and making this talent unavailable for projects that offer real potential for economic growth. The wasteful expenditure of construction materials, labor and equipment limit the useful projects that can be pursued. Other "EARMARKS" give political cronies an advantage over their competition, thus raising your cost of living and limiting your opportunities.

Individual freedom (CAPITALISM) selects projects based upon the belief that the project will produce wealth. "EARMARKS" are selected to reward political cronies or create new cronies for support in the next election. The effect of "EARMARKS" is to increase the personal power or the personal wealth of the "WANNABE PEERS" that propose them.

There are many instances of politicians and others listing questionable or ridiculous "EARMARKS". It would serve no purpose to list more of the waste and corruption here. "EARMARKS" are more of a threat to individual freedom than the price tag indicates.

CHAPTER ELEVEN

THE INCOME TAX

A progressive income tax is an integral and necessary part of the "WANNABE PEERS'" program to regain the wealth and prestige the "PEERS" enjoyed under King George III.

As originally adopted, the Constitution limited the power of Congress to enact direct taxes by requiring that direct taxes be imposed in proportion to the State's Census population. Article 1, Section 8, Clause 1 of the Constitution states:**"No Capitation, or other direct, Tax shall be laid, unless in proportion to the Census or enumeration herein before directed to be taken"**. Nevertheless, the Revenue Act of 1861 imposed an income tax of 3% on all income over $800. That first income tax was enacted to pay the cost of the Civil War expense. The Act was revised in 1862 and finally repealed in 1872. However, the 1894 Tariff Act instituted a new income tax. The Supreme Court found the new tax unconstitutional but the victory was short-lived. "WANNABE PEERS" were successful in having the 16th Amendment to the Constitution ratified in 1913 removing the constitutional prohibition of the income tax. The 16th Amendment was sold to the public on the basis that it would only tax the rich. The Revenue

Act of 1913 imposed a personal income tax. The act levied a 1% tax on personal income above $3,000 and a 6% surtax on an income over a half million dollars. Because of inflation, a $3000 income in **1913** is the equivalent of $75,000 in 2008. The original income tax law applied to less than 1% of the population and the "WANNABE PEERS" gained political support by oppressing their chosen enemy, the "RICH" (successful "COMMONS"). Those who thought that the income tax would never apply to them were in for one big surprise. The income tax very quickly became very progressive to finance the First World War. The maximum tax rate was raised to 77% of all income over one million dollars and the minimum rate was lowered to 2% on all income over $2000. In 1952 and 1953, the maximum income tax rate reached a peak of 92% on income over $400,000. Cooler heads prevailed, and by 2003 the peak income tax rate was reduced to 35 percent of the income over $307,050.

A high tax rate (as high as 92%) on a fast-growing business has a devastating effect on the "COMMONS'" ability to expand their business. The tax made it impossible to internally generate capital required for expansion and very difficult to obtain capital from investors.

The typical "COMMON" (entrepreneur) works long hours to create the wealth required for expanding the business. Of course, if the government confiscates that wealth it is not available to expand the business. The progressive income tax is analogous to the farmer feeding his seed corn to the chickens to increase the production of manure. If wealth the "COMMON" creates is confiscated,

201

the capital required to grow the business must be obtained from other sources. If the entrepreneur accepts capital investment, he loses some of the control of his business. The loss of control affects the ability of the "COMMON" to make business decisions and sometimes leads to loss of control of the business. Of course, the threat of confiscation of the wealth by the government reduces the "COMMONS'" incentive to produce that wealth and makes it more difficult to obtain capital from investors. That lack of incentive and availability of capital slows or stops the growth of the "technology dividend".

There is considerable risk involved when investing in a new or unproven business. Because of the risk involved, the investor expects to recoup his original investment in less than five years and earn a profit of at least 15% per year. If the business is a corporation and is taxed at a 50% rate, the investor will require a projected profit of over 30 percent in addition to recouping the original investment in less than five years.

Such a profit requirement makes it very difficult to justify an investment in any new and/or unproven business. Only the best of the best could qualify. The "WANNABE PEERS" would have you believe that corporate income taxes are paid by corporations. A "for-profit" corporation's only source of revenue is from the sale of its products. Corporate taxes are simply another cost of doing business and must be included in the cost of the company's products. Ultimately the taxes are paid by the corporation's customers. The effect of corporate income taxes and taxes on the entrepreneur simply makes it more difficult to obtain capital for new and unproven businesses and increases the cost of the businesses' products to the consumer.

Income tax, especially the progressive income tax, is a direct assault on the "technology dividend" and is a big factor in maintaining the "status quo". In addition, it eliminates the "COMMONS'" (entrepreneur) incentive to create wealth.

The income tax is not a tax on the rich. It's a tax on productivity. The very "RICH" simply want to maintain the "status quo" and prevent new technology from destroying the value of their mature business or threatening their dominance in the market place. Remember, it was the very rich "WANNABE PEERS" that financed both Hitler's and Mussolini's quest for power. Limiting the "COMMONS'" (entrepreneur) access to capital can:

- Prevent new products and services from being offered in the marketplace (benefiting the "WANNABE PEERS'" supporters in maintaining the "status quo" and preventing growth in the "technology dividend").

- Force the entrepreneur to yield control of his business to the established competitor.

- Force the "COMMON" into bankruptcy.

The "WANNABE PEERS" routinely change the tax laws to benefit other "WANNABE PEERS" and "PAWNS" to obtain their political support. These changes continue to complicate the tax code. Between 1955 and 2005 the number of words in the tax code[64] increased by over 425 percent (from 409,000 to 2,139,000 words) and the increase continues today. This increasing complexity of the tax code has caused a corresponding increase in the cost of complying with the tax code as well as the risk of violating it.

The "TAX FOUNDATION'S" special report[64], "THE RISING COST OF COMPLYING WITH FEDERAL INCOME TAX", estimates that the cost of complying with The Federal Income Tax Code increased 305 percent between 1990 and 2005 (from $79.7 billion in 1990 to $243.9 billion in 2004). In the same report, the actual cost to the income taxpayer of complying with the income tax code in 2004 was $1.24 for each dollar of revenue collected by the government. Compliance costs on new and small businesses with little or no profit is a cost to the business that greatly exceeds the revenue collected and consumes the businesses' assets that otherwise would be available for growth. Income tax compliance cost on a growing business with little or no profits is a direct assault on the "technology dividend".

The estimate of the cost of income tax compliance in this report does not include the cost for tax planning or tax audit and litigation costs. The cost of operating the Internal Revenue Service is not included. So this estimate is much lower than the actual cost the income tax places on the economy. The complexity of the tax code has continued to increase since 2004 but this report proves the point. Of course, time and effort spent to comply with the tax code and protect one's wealth from the tax man is nonproductive work and that effort is unavailable to expand the business and create wealth. Both the taxes paid and the compliance cost has a devastating effect on the "technology dividend" and the economy.

Considering the high cost of collecting the income tax, can anyone seriously believe that the real purpose of the income tax is to raise revenue for the government? The purpose of income tax is to allow the "WANNABE PEERS" to gain political advantage by appearing to punish their chosen enemy, the "RICH", and to use the power of the IRS to control political dissent and extort political support.

The complexity[64] of the income tax laws makes it almost impossible to determine one's obligation. How do you comply with something you can't even identify? A long enough investigation of almost any business will turn up a failure to comply with some obscure requirement in the tax code. Even if the investigation fails to turn up a violation, the investigation can cost the "COMMON" (entrepreneur) both wealth and considerable time: wealth and time that "COMMONS" could use to create wealth. Just the threat of an investigation allows "WANNABE PEERS" to control their political opponents or extort political support from "COMMONS".

The first use of the income tax for purposes other than obtaining government revenue was an attack on the gangsters created by the government's ill fated experiment with Prohibition. When the 18th Amendment to the Constitution was enacted, distribution of alcohol became illegal and the criminal element rushed in to fill the void. The illegal distribution of alcohol was extremely lucrative and the criminal element was able to bribe local government officials, making local prosecution of prohibition offenses very difficult, if not impossible. Criminal gangs in the Chicago area fought for control of alcohol distribution. Gun fights became commonplace on the streets, fueling public outrage. Because of corruption of public officials and witnesses' fear of testifying against the criminals, it was almost impossible to successfully prosecute the well-connected criminals. The Federal Government used the income tax laws to successfully prosecute these well-connected criminals. Although the conviction on income tax charges resulted in collection of taxes, the primary purpose of the prosecution was to remove a dangerous criminal element from the streets.

The government could hardly be faulted for using whatever tools were available to rid the streets of these criminals. However, it was the first use of the income tax for purposes other than collecting revenue.

The power of the IRS would soon be used for less ethical purposes.

THE "WANNABE PEERS" USE OF THE IRS AGAINST POLITICAL ENEMIES:

Many of our Presidents have used the power of the Internal Revenue Service against their political opponents.

Herbert Hoover was the first to use the IRS against political enemies. President Hoover ordered the secret FBI investigation[65] of an organization called "Weapons Manufacturers". The investigation was partially based on confidential tax information supplied by the IRS.

Elliott Roosevelt[35] made the following statement about his father, President Roosevelt (FDR), "my father may have been the originator of the concept of employing the IRS as a weapon of political retribution." President Roosevelt's first target using the IRS was Louisiana's Huey Long.

Huey Long was a thorn in the side of President Roosevelt until he was assassinated. Mr. Roosevelt tried various ways to control Mr. Long. None were very successful until he came up with the idea of using the Internal Revenue Service. Mr. Long protested on the floor of the Senate that the IRS sent at least 250 agents into Louisiana to investigate him and his supporters. In 1935, the IRS began prosecuting the more vulnerable (openly corrupt) of Mr. Long's supporters; however, before the IRS was ready to prosecute Mr. Long he was assassinated. Trying to end the prosecutions, Mr. Long's political heirs agreed to support President Roosevelt's reelection campaign in return for having the pending charges dropped. Mr. Long's political machine provided President Roosevelt with 90% of the Louisiana votes in the 1936 election. After the election, the IRS did prosecute a few of the worst offenders; so the first use of the IRS power against political opponents was extremely successful, if somewhat unethical.

There is no doubt that Mr. Long was a corrupt politician and deserved to be prosecuted. However, he was selected for prosecution, not because of the corruption but because of his opposition to President Roosevelt. For instance, Frank Hague, a political boss in Jersey City, was just as corrupt a politician as Mr. Long. However, Mr. Hague supported President Roosevelt, and he received considerable federal patronage for this effort. Even though the IRS had considerable evidence of his corruption, he was never prosecuted. When told that the IRS planned to prosecute Mr. Hague[25], President Roosevelt said **"Forget prosecution. You go tell Frank to knock it off. We can't have this kind of thing going on. But keep this quiet. We need Hague's support if we want to win New Jersey."**

President Roosevelt instigated many IRS investigations against other political enemies. Elliott Roosevelt is quoted as saying **"other men's tax returns continued to fascinate Father in the [nineteen] thirties."** At President Roosevelt's (FDR) direction the IRS investigated William Randolph Hearst, the newspaper publisher, Father Charles Coughlin, host of a religious radio program in Detroit, Boake Carter, another radio commentator, and Hamilton Fish, a Republican congressman from New York State, just to name a few. But in the 1930's, income tax laws were not as complex as they are today and the targets had good accounting practices. Mr. Roosevelt's attempts to use the IRS to silence media personalities were unsuccessful. No evidence of corruption was turned up on Hamilton Fish.

It is not the results of these attempts to use the IRS against political enemies; it is the fact that the attempts were made, that is important. When government force is used against an individual for political purposes, our freedom is in peril.

No evidence could be found that President Eisenhower or President Truman used the IRS against their political enemies.

Although the director of the IRS denied that Pres. Kennedy used the IRS against political opponents, there is some evidence that he ordered the IRS to investigate some right wing organizations. David Burnham's statement[65] before the Senate Finance Committee states as follows:

"With the full knowledge of President Kennedy and his brother, the IRS Commissioner of that administration established a program to go after "extremist organizations." Although the memos describing the program said the extremists of concern were on both the right and the left, it appears that all of those who lost their tax exempt status in connection with this program were "fundamentalist conservatives who had been criticizing the President." If true, this was a direct attack on a political opponent using the full force of the federal government. If there were no income tax, "TAX EXEMPT STATUS" would have no meaning and this type of intimidation would be impossible.

President Lyndon Johnson[66] tried to control information disseminated by churches, by threatening their tax exempt status.

President Nixon[65] established the "Special Services Staff" "SSS" in the IRS. The purpose of the "SSS" was to use tax records to track "dissident groups and individuals" (President Nixon's political enemies). One of the impeachment counts approved by the "House Judiciary Committee" involved President Nixon's use of the IRS against his political enemies. President Nixon's abuse of the IRS powers may have been even worse than that of FDR.

The more recent abuses have been left to the reader's imagination. No purpose is served by delving into the more recent abuses that may involve the reader's emotions making an objective evaluation more difficult. These historical examples proved beyond a shadow of a doubt that the "WANNABE PEERS" have used the IRS to silence and oppress their political opposition. This practice continues even though the evidence is not included in this book.

SUMMARY:

Income tax makes it more difficult to obtain capital for new businesses and unproven businesses. There's no way to determine the products and technology that have been left undeveloped because of the failure to obtain capital because of income tax.

The effect of the income tax on the "technology dividend" has been considerable, even though there is no way to identify the actual cost to the economy and your standard of living.

Selective investigation and enforcement of the income tax laws by the IRS at the direction the "WANNABE PEERS" provide the means to destroy political opposition and is a direct assault on your freedom. It can also be used by the "WANNABE PEERS" to reward "PAWNS" and obtain political support at your expense.

Lobbying efforts to obtain special exemptions, exceptions and deductions in the income tax laws are a source of political support and campaign funds for the "WANNABE PEERS".

The income tax is a perfect fit in the "WANNABE PEERS" agenda to regain the power and prestige that "PEERS" enjoyed under KING GEORGE III.

CHAPTER TWELVE

THE WAY BACK

For over 100 years "WANNABE PEERS" have used the preponderance of propaganda to convince the American people that the benevolent coercion of the Government would provide a better life if only they would surrender their freedom for the false promise of security and unearned wealth. The first 11 chapters of this book proved conclusively that individual freedom is the key to prosperity, not government coercion. The fact is that Government coercion can only lead to poverty and injustice. Five of the "WANNABE PEERS" "show case" programs, THE SHERMAN ANTITRUST ACT, THE BUREAUCRACY-ICC, INFLATION, EARMARKS and INCOME TAX, were selected for analysis because each has a long history (some over 100 years). The effects of these programs are well documented in history so the facts cannot be disputed. The advantage of using historical programs is that these programs are free of the emotion incited by the preponderance of propaganda used to expand the "WANNABE PEERS" agenda. The "WANNABE PEERS", secure in the belief that these five programs have general public acceptance, no longer tout these programs with the preponderance of propaganda. These five programs are

211

historical centerpieces of the "WANNABE PEERS" agenda and exhibit all of the fallacies of government coercion. All five programs were shown, conclusively, to destroy individual liberty and wealth. All these programs created poverty instead of prosperity, misery instead of wellbeing. Both human history and the analysis of these programs prove that freedom creates prosperity while oppression (government coercion) destroys wealth and increases poverty. This proof means that if a program limits individual freedom, it must also destroy wealth and create poverty. Once you have determined that the program limits individual freedom, that program can be condemned without determining exactly how or why the program destroys wealth and creates poverty. A war or other crisis can make a temporary restriction of individual freedom necessary to protect our country from its enemies.

Do not expect the "WANNABE PEERS" to accept this logical analysis of their programs. The preponderance of propaganda routinely ignores and misrepresents facts that do not support the "WANNABE PEERS" position. The preponderance of propaganda only publicizes facts that either support the "WANNABE PEERS" agenda or spins the meaning of those facts to support their agenda. An unbiased review of the results of these five programs leaves no doubt that each of these programs attacks individual freedom, destroys wealth, increases poverty and limits the growth of the "technology dividend".

Either the "WANNABE PEERS" are incredibly naïve or their long-term purpose is to create the economic crisis that will culminate in a totalitarian government.

The "WANNABE PEERS" have enacted many programs that suppress freedom and are proposing many more. Many of these new programs are just as destructive as the five programs analyzed in Chapters 7 through 11 and build on the base provided by these five programs. It is tempting to explain the fallacies of these programs and proposals but it would only complicate the book. Sufficient proof has been presented to validate the principles and conclusions that freedom creates prosperity and coercion creates poverty. If the reader disagrees with these conclusions and principles, more specific information on the results of more of the "WANNABE PEERS'" programs will not sway that opinion. Besides, the reader who rejects this logic and reasoning probably stopped reading after the first chapter. The reader who understands the principles and conclusions put forth in this book will have no problem understanding and rejecting the "WANNABE PEERS" false promises of security and unearned wealth. More specifics on the effects of other programs and current proposals would just be a waste of time.

Four of the five programs, in addition to creating poverty and destroying individual freedom, allow the "WANNABE PEERS" to use government force to oppress political enemies and coerce the individual to support their agenda. The "WANNABE PEERS" have the power to financially destroy or even jail political opponents and this power will make recovering our freedom very difficult. Unless the "WANNABE PEERS" can be stripped of this power

213

to destroy the political opposition, reversing the trend that is destroying your individual freedom will be impossible. If the financial destruction isn't enough; criminal prosecution is available to the IRS in tax evasion cases. Even though the author of this book has been retired for over 10 years and has had almost no income during that period, you can bet that he will be the target of an IRS audit, if this book is successful. If this book is very, very successful, the preponderance of propaganda will attack the writer's character with the expectation that exposing character flaws will somehow invalidate the facts, logic and the conclusions presented in this book.

It took over 100 years to create this mess and an instantaneous solution is not possible. The change must be slow and methodical to avoid the crisis that is the "WANNABE PEERS" objective. To regain our freedom, we will have to exercise patience just as the "WANNABE PEERS" have exercised patience for over 100 years to usurp our freedom.

The use of force and violence would only create the crisis that the "WANNABE PEERS" have worked for. That crisis would cause chaos allowing a "WANNABE KING" to seize power by restoring order. There will not be another GEORGE WASHINGTON who refuses the crown. Instead, the "WANNABE KING" will promise to "maintain order until stability can be maintained and provide free elections within 18 months". At least that is the promise Castro made to Cuba in the "MANIFESTO OF THE SIERRA MAESTRA[17]". Of course, Cuba is still waiting for those free elections. Widespread armed confrontation between our citizens and the government can only result in the establishment of a totalitarian government and the "WANNABE PEERS" (perhaps not those in control at the start of the conflict) will win by default.

The "preponderance of propaganda" is a master of misdirection as well as misinformation. To regain our freedom, it will be necessary to maintain focus on a narrow set of objectives; do not let the "WANNABE PEERS" use emotional issues to move your attention to irrelevant, but emotionally charged issues. The use of issues, such as entitlement programs, invoke strong emotions with people concerned about loafers consuming unearned wealth and others concerned about the survival and suffering of the indigent.

Instances of government provided welfare[12] have been with us since the late Tenth Century. The simple fact is that we simply will not allow our fellow citizens to die of malnutrition and exposure in the streets. Some form of welfare will be with us because of the inherent compassion most people feel toward our fellow citizens. In 1776, it took long hours (forty acres and a mule) to produce the bare necessities of life. Any wealth expended on the indigent was a severe drain on the economy.

The "WANNABE PEERS" still point to the long work hours required to produce the wealth for survival in the late Nineteenth and early Twentieth Century as exploitation of the worker. It was not exploitation of the worker that caused the long work hours; it was lower individual productivity. Today, the cost to the economy of providing adequate food and shelter is minimal. Between the years 1900

215

and 2000 the percent of the workforce employed
in agriculture[67] declined from 41 percent to
1.9 percent. Even with that low percentage
working in agriculture, 91 percent of the
farmers only farm part time. In the year
2000, the portion of the GDP (gross domestic
product) produced by agriculture was only 0.7
percent of the total United States' GDP[67].
The average growth per year of the "technology
dividend" over the last fifty years was 2.13
percent. Properly administered, the cost to
the economy of providing a safety net would
not exceed the deflationary effect of the
technology dividend. This assumes that we are
successful in regaining our freedom and
removing the regulatory brakes from the
economy. The ambition created by the renewed
freedom will leave few people content to
accept the bare subsistence offered by a
safety net and those trapped there will work
to regain a place in productive society. The
issue of entitlements will solve itself when
freedom is restored.

Along with touting entitlement issues,
the preponderance of propaganda will continue
to try to play special interest groups against
each other and the general population. The
"WANNABE PEERS" will continue to attack their
chosen enemy, the rich. Ignore these
distractions. Remember, only individuals have
rights and any special rights provided to
special interests must first be taken from the
individual. The "WANNABE PEERS" enemy,
defined as the "RICH", is not really the rich.
The "WANNABE PEERS" enemy is the "COMMONS"
(producer) and harassment of the producer is
not in the best interest of the consumer.

The important objective is to regain our freedom. If we fail to regain our freedom, we will all be on the government dole but there will be little or nothing for the "WANNABE PEERS" to distribute.

The entitlement issue, special rights for special interests and harassment of the "WANNABE PEERS" chosen enemy are just distractions and must be ignored. The purpose of the preponderance of propaganda on these issues is simply to induce you to make emotional decisions to surrender more of your freedom.

HOW DO WE GET OUT OF THIS MESS?
THE SOLUTION TO POLITICALLY MOTIVATED PROSECUTION:

As long as the "WANNABE PEERS" have the power to financially destroy and/or incarcerate political opponents[35, 63, 64, 65, 66], they will have the power to neutralize any effective opposition. The income tax code and other bureaucratic rules and regulations are all attacks on individual freedom. Yet it is not these programs that are the greatest danger to our freedom. The greatest danger to the Republic is the "WANNABE PEERS" use of the IRS and other bureaucracies to investigate and prosecute political enemies. Serious attempts to reverse the assaults on individual freedom or replace the income tax will be suicide while the "WANNABE PEERS" retain the power to use the IRS and other bureaucracies to investigate and prosecute their political enemies. Even without the use of force by the bureaucracy, the "politics of personal destruction" represented by the "WANNABE PEERS" control of the preponderance of propaganda is a serious obstacle.

217

CHAPTER 12

The "WANNABE PEERS" use of regulatory agencies and the IRS to control or destroy their political enemies get very little, if any, press coverage. Most of the instances uncovered by the research for this book were documented long after the crime and by then it was old news. Do not discount the danger simply because it is ignored by the media.

Since 1977 most of the information on "WANNABE PEERS" political use of the IRS[68] involves investigations of tax exempt organizations' political activities against the "WANNABE PEERS" in power. The objective was to silence the dissent by eliminating the favorable tax treatment extended to charitable, non-profit and religious organizations.

There was also some information concerning use of the IRS against personal enemies of the President.

"WHAT DO YOU EXPECT WHEN YOU SUE THE PRESIDENT?" Paul Breslan[70], a senior IRS official, told the "JUDICIAL WATCH", a Washington-based legal watchdog group that had filed over 50 legal actions against the Clinton administration and was under investigation by the IRS. This audit of "JUDICIAL WATCH" was in 1998. Apparently this "senior" IRS official believed that it was the duty of the IRS to audit (prosecute) the President's political enemies. Did you really think the only purpose of the IRS was just to collect taxes? Just the threat of retaliation by the IRS has a chilling effect on potential dissenters.

The extent to which the IRS is used against political enemies of the "WANNABE PEERS" in recent history is probably understated in this book. Much of President Roosevelt's unethical, if not criminal use of the IRS did not become public until well over 10 years after his death. The threat exists and even if the use is not fully documented for the recent past, that threat must be removed before an effective campaign to regain our freedom can succeed.

The purpose of this book is to document and prove this grave threat to regaining our freedom, not to judge or demonize past Presidents. The evidence clearly shows that for over 75 years some of our Presidents have used the power of the IRS to retaliate against political opponents and even personal enemies. Generally, the purpose was to control and even eliminate political dissent. While one would hope that a person who achieved the Presidency of the United States would be above such unethical practices, it is not the Presidents that are to blame.

The blame belongs to a system that permits such abuses of government power. We cannot expect "WANNABE PEERS" to forego such an opportunity to enhance their personal power when the system offers that opportunity.

The IRS, while perhaps the most widely used bureaucracy to control political dissent, is not the only source of abuse. Any government agency that possesses the power to create rules and regulations and enforce those rules and regulations as investigator, prosecutor, judge and jury can be used for the same purpose. While these bureaucracies have considerable power, it is generally only useful against the more successful "COMMONS", not the individual. The ability of a bureaucracy to make and enforce rules and regulations without congressional action or oversight by the courts, presents a powerful force to control political dissent by successful "COMMONS" (producers).

An accused criminal has more protection from malicious prosecution than the political dissenter or the "COMMONS" (producer) whose only crime is the attempt to create wealth. To prosecute an alleged criminal, an indictment requiring some proof of violation of the law, is required. For the IRS to audit a victim, only a hint from a powerful "WANNABE PEER" is required. Make no mistake about it; an IRS audit is a prosecution except that the IRS acts as both judge and jury. An IRS audit can easily result in criminal prosecution and the whole process can easily cost more than the alleged tax liability even if the victim prevails. If the victim does prevail, nothing prevents the IRS from finding another alleged violation to audit, unlike the criminal who is protected by "double jeopardy".

How on earth did we get ourselves in such a mess? Even more important, how do we regain our freedom?

Of course, abolishing the IRS and all the other bureaucracies would also abolish the abuses of power described above but such an abrupt change in conditions would certainly result in chaos. Besides, such a law would never be passed by the Congress and if it were to pass, the President would certainly veto it. Even though the system has many faults it does maintain order and secures the wealth required to operate the government.

A campaign to restore individual freedom cannot be effective while the "WANNABE PEERS" have the ability to use the power of the government to punish and silence political dissent.

ELIMINATION OF THE ABILITY OF THE "WANNABE PEERS" TO USE THE POWER OF THE GOVERNMENT TO PROSECUTE AND DESTROY POLITICAL OPPOSITION HAS TO BE THE FIRST PRIORITY OF ANY EFFORT TO REVERSE THE TREND THAT IS DESTROYING OUR FREEDOM AND PROSPERITY.

Make no mistake about it; the "WANNABE PEERS" will use all their power and the preponderance of propaganda to maintain a system that allows them to use government force to stifle political dissent. The first step to diminish that power will have to be small and so popular that the "WANNABE PEERS" will not dare to openly oppose it. Not even the most resourceful "WANNABE PEER" would try to justify selection of the bureaucrats' targets based upon political activity of the victim.

Their arguments will be that any restriction or requirement to justify the selection of the bureaucrat's target will cost too much and reduce the efficiency of the bureaucracy.

The first objective in the agenda to regain our freedom must be to establish a "PERMANENT INDEPENDENT COUNSEL", with full prosecutorial and subpoena power to investigate the selection of the bureaucrat's victims. If one claimed to be the victim of a political vendetta, the Independent Counsel would require that the prosecution of the victim be suspended until the Independent Counsel's investigation was complete and had proven beyond a reasonable doubt that valid probable cause for the investigation was possessed by the bureaucrat prior to initiating the prosecution. If the probable cause were invalid the Independent Counsel would have the duty to start both criminal and civil action against the responsible perpetrator (bureaucrat and/or wannabe peer).

To create an Independent Counsel with the power to eliminate the potential for this misuse of power will require a massive "grass roots" effort. Perhaps this book will inspire a freedom orientated PAC (political action committee) to champion the cause and provide the leadership to remove this source of power (persecution of political enemies) from the "WANNABE PEERS" arsenal. If there were ever a cause that transcends party lines, this is it. There is no other issue with both broad emotional and intellectual appeal as political persecution. PACS live on donations and the potential for donations for this cause cannot be underestimated. Perhaps a PAC will see the potential and champion this cause.

When this proposal is introduced, the "WANNABE PEERS" will try to amend the proposed law to eliminate its effectiveness while claiming to support the objective. Do not let them fool you; your freedom depends on it! It is not the efficiency of the bureaucracy that is important. Your freedom and above all, justice, is the important objective.

There is nothing that poses a greater threat to the REPUBLIC and your freedom than the "WANNABE PEERS" ability to prosecute political dissenters! It won't be easy to obtain this first objective but until "WANNABE PEERS" power to prosecute political enemies is eliminated; any effort to regain our freedom is doomed to failure.

Once the "WANNABE PEERS" power to prosecute political opponents has been ended, the next grave threat to our freedom is the power of the bureaucracy to act as legislator, investigator, prosecutor, judge and jury.
ELIMINATE THE BUREAUCRACY:

The bureaucracy is a fourth branch of the Government created by the Congress to escape the blame for its actions. Establishing a powerful Independent Counsel will add protection to the individual from malicious prosecution for political activity but considerable potential still exists for the "WANNABE PEERS" to use the bureaucracy to eliminate opposition and extort support from "COMMONS". If the leaders of industry (particularly new or fast growing industry) are effectively silenced, it threatens the freedom of all and presents a threat to the "technology dividend".

Total elimination of this fourth branch of government is necessary to secure our freedom! Again, we must exercise patience. Although these rules and regulations and the enforcement mechanism have a destructive effect on the economy, stability must be maintained. Sudden removal of the bureaucracy would cause chaos and crisis. The economic crisis that the "WANNABE PEERS" have been seeking might well result. Some of those rules and regulations may be necessary and should not be discarded without evaluation. Remember the "iron triangle" described in Chapter 8. Most of these regulations were the result of "WANNABE PEERS" seeking power and "PAWNS" seeking personal gain at the expense of the "COMMONS".

CHAPTER 12

   Dismantling this fourth branch of
government must be done carefully and any
necessary functions preserved to avoid chaos.
Functions and powers that present the greatest
threat to our freedom must go first.

   A basic tenet of our law was that the
accused was innocent until proven guilty in a
court of law. This started to change with the
"HEPBURN ACT OF 1906". Congress gave the
Interstate Commerce Commission (ICC) the power
to set railroad freight rates that were
"reasonable and just" (after a full hearing)
and placed the "burden of proof" on the
accused (the railroads). To undo the ICC's
decision, the railroads had to prove in court
that the ICC was wrong (the railroads were
guilty until proven innocent). Congress has
continued to increase the power of the
bureaucracy since that time.

   The police must have "probable cause" and
obtain a warrant from the judicial branch to
go into an accused criminal's home and search
for evidence. The bureaucrat only has to walk
into the "COMMONS" business and demand access
and cooperation. The accused criminal has
more rights than the "COMMONS" (producer).
Bureaucrats (from several agencies) can enter
and investigate a business without "probable
cause" or a warrant. The bureaucrats have the
power to levy fines for what they consider
infractions of their regulations. If the
"WANNABE PEERS" want to pressure a "COMMON"
and the bureaucrats fail to find an
infraction, they can create new regulations
that are sure to be violated, giving the
"WANNABE PEERS" the leverage needed to extort
support or control the actions of the
"COMMONS". To create new regulations, the

224

bureaucrats might be inconvenienced by having to hold a "public hearing", causing a slight delay and giving the bureaucrat another excuse to increase their budget. The new regulations can be swiftly enforced and the "COMMONS" destroyed, while the "WANNABE PEERS" and their "PAWNS" feed on the corpse. If the disaster caused by the bureaucrats becomes public knowledge, the "WANNABE PEERS" can always condemn the "out of control bureaucrats" and gain political support by promising to correct the problem.

The fourth branch of the government must go the way of the Dodo[39] bird if we are to regain our freedom! The bureaucracy must be incrementally stripped of power until it becomes irrelevant and can be eliminated. The action to provide the "COMMONS" with relief from the oppression of each agency should be in the following order:

- The most dangerous power of the bureaucracy is the ability to levy fines. That power would be replaced with the requirement that infractions that could not be resolved by negotiation between the agency and the "COMMONS" be referred to the Justice Department for prosecution. The "COMMONS" would retain the "presumption of innocence" until convicted in a court of law. How quaint, giving the "COMMONS" the same rights as an accused criminal!

- The power to enter a business without consent of the business would be the next to be deleted. The bureaucrat would be required to obtain a warrant to enter the premises if access is denied. "Probable Cause" of an infraction would be required to obtain the warrant. More equality

225

between the "COMMONS" and the accused criminal!

- The bureaucrat's "conflict of interest" in proposing new regulations must be recognized and neutralized. The bureaucracy's prime objective is to increase its budget – new regulations support a budget increase. The bureaucrats would not be allowed to either propose or create new regulations.

- Each agency would be required to submit to Congress a detailed "ECONOMIC IMPACT STATEMENT" on each active regulation. If Congress failed to approve the "ECONOMIC IMPACT STATEMENT" within ninety days of the submission and write the regulation into law, regulation would be discarded. A detailed "ECONOMIC IMPACT STATEMENT" would be required and approved by Congress before Congress could vote on any new law.

- Transfer the power to prosecute and investigate infractions to the Justice Department.

Once these steps were completed, the agency would be irrelevant and could be abolished. New regulations could not be enacted without congressional approval of an "Economic Impact Statement" and the passage of the law by the Congress. The "WANNABE PEERS" will be quick to point out that congressional committees study the legislation so an "Economic Impact Statement" is not necessary. History shows that the Congressional committee has not protected the "COMMONS" or our individual freedom. Any law that affects the economy should be subject to periodic "Economic Impact Statements" requiring

Congressional approval to continue the law. Congress could not blame the bureaucracy for the failure of the bureaucrat's policies and the requirement for an "ECONOMIC IMPACT STATEMENT" would prevent Congress from claiming ignorance of the consequences of legislative action. Approval of an "ECONOMIC IMPACT STATEMENT" prior to voting on the legislation would prevent the congressional leadership from passing legislation that has unknown provisions.

THE INCOME TAX:

Once the "WANNABE PEERS'" use of the IRS to punish political dissenters has been eliminated, some of the support for the income tax may disappear. However, the income tax is a terrible drain on the economy and increasing poverty is a necessary part of the WANNABE PEERS'" strategy. In addition to making it more difficult to obtain capital to fund new projects, the cost[64] (2004) to corporations of complying with IRS regulations was almost 25 percent of the tax paid. Since 2004 much complexity has been added to the income tax regulations, so the 25 percent figure is probably significantly understated for today's economy. This means that compliance with the IRS regulations causes corporations to expend non-productive labor with an average value of at least 25 percent of the income tax paid. This is an average figure and the compliance cost (as a percent of taxes) would be much more for small growing companies with little or no profit. For a start-up company the compliance cost is a nonproductive expense that increases the cost of doing business. Of course, this cost must be passed on to the consumer. The compliance cost for IRS regulations is a direct assault on the "technology dividend". The income tax must be replaced with a more equitable tax system to allow growth of the technology dividend and achieve the prosperity that capitalism can provide.

EARMARKS:

The requirement that Congress approve an "Economic Impact Statement" before it could pass a new law should end the "EARMARK" problem.

INFLATION:

Once the inflation of currency is recognized as a tax, the required "Economic Impact Statement" on the Federal budget should solve the inflation problem. If the long term inflation of the currency were equal to the growth of the "technology dividend", a stable value to the dollar would be achieved.

SHERMAN ANTITRUST ACT:

It is virtually impossible to determine the economic damage that has resulted from the Sherman Antitrust act. It should be repealed immediately. The elimination of the bureaucracy will only add small inconveniences to the "WANNABE PEERS" enforcement of the antitrust laws. The ability of the "WANNABE PEERS" to protect politically powerful but "technologically challenged" political supporters from innovators and punish successful "COMMONS" must be ended. Prosperity demands that the "technology dividend" be set free from the "emergency brake" applied by the Sherman Antitrust Act.

Repealing the Antitrust Laws will not be easy. The "WANNABE PEERS" will warn of the dangers of an economic monopoly. The truth is that a monopoly has never had an extended life unless it was supported by the use of force and the government has the monopoly on force. An effective tactic might be to apply the Antitrust Laws to government enforced monopolies. The post office, labor unions and public education certainly violate the Sherman Antitrust Act and would be prime targets. These three examples have a much more detrimental effect on the consumer than a company like Microsoft adding features to its product that limit competitors' ability to sell that feature. The purpose of the tactic is not to actually apply the law to these monopolies. The purpose is to repeal the Sherman Antitrust Law.

OTHER GOVERNMENT ABUSES TO INDIVIDUAL LIBERTY:

- Victimless crimes[71] are laws that attempt to control individual behavior but do not create a victim when the crime is violated. Examples are controlled substances laws, laws against prostitution and public decency. These "victimless crimes" have a tremendous economic cost. According to Peter McWilliams' book, "AIN'T NOBODY'S BUSINESS IF YOU DO", over 350,000 people are incarcerated for "victimless crimes" and 1,500,000 more are on parole or probation, their earning capacity forever diminished by a felony conviction. $50 billion will be spent to punish victimless crime offenses and $150 billion will be lost in tax revenue. The cost to the economy is probably much greater than the estimates. Some estimates show that fully one-third of the United State's agricultural GDP[72] is marijuana, an illegal substance. The cost to the economy is staggering. The cost in human misery is even greater. Would ending the recreational use of marijuana and other drugs be desirable? Perhaps, but it is not the government's decision. It is the individual's decision. Did we learn nothing from the experiment with prohibition? The cure is worse than the disease. "Victimless crimes" destroy wealth and increase poverty and that increases the "WANNABE PEERS" constituency. So don't expect any help on changing the "victimless crime" laws from the "WANNABE PEERS". The consequences of the "victimless crime" laws advance the "WANNABE PEERS'" agenda.

- **GOVERNMENT AND THE EMPLOYER AND EMPLOYEE RELATIONSHIP:**

    Governmental meddling in the relationship between the employer and employee increases the cost of all "consumable assets" and "active assets". This meddling is simply an attempt by the "WANNABE PEERS" to obtain political support from powerful pressure groups and "PAWNS" by using the government's monopoly on force to redistribute wealth at a terrible cost to the economy and individual freedom. A complete evaluation of the cost and injustice caused by the government's intrusion into the relationship between the employer and employee would fill a book of its own. The requirement for an "Economic Impact Statement" might eliminate this problem.

- **ENVIRONMENTAL REGULATIONS:**

Environmental regulations based upon emotional arguments with no basis in fact and total disregard for the economic consequences have had a devastating effect on the economy. The destruction of wealth by many current regulations pale when compared to the economic consequences of using government force to limit carbon dioxide emissions. Serious consideration has never been given to a program that has more potential to:

o Reduce individual freedom.
o Destroy more wealth.
o Redistribute more wealth to the "WANNABE PEERS" and their supporters.
o Create more poverty and increase the "WANNABE PEERS'" constituency.

The bogus claim[6, 7] that carbon dioxide emissions cause "global warming" is supported only by emotional claims of disaster if we don't act immediately. No valid proof is offered that carbon dioxide emissions have any effect on climate change.

The "ENERGY ALCHEMIST" touting "alternative energy" won't tell you that the difference between "alternative energy" and "primary energy" is that "alternative energy" costs more. Remember, all "consumable assets" have energy content. Any increase in the cost of energy increases the cost of living and creates poverty. The increase in the cost of living due to elimination or reduction of carbon dioxide emissions will make almost everyone dependent upon the government for subsistence. Without carbon dioxide emissions, the government will have little to distribute.

The cost of "alternative energy", touted by the "ENERGY ALCHEMIST" will be devastating to the consumer and create wide spread poverty at levels we never dreamed of, even in the "great depression". The destruction of the economy, resulting from elimination or reduction of carbon dioxide emissions will surely produce the "WANNABE PEERS" final objective, the "economic crisis" that gives them total control. Even those who expect to profit from the elimination of carbon dioxide emissions will find that the wealth received by virtue of this attack on civilization has little or no value.

Many books[6], [7] have been written on this subject and more are being written today. The subject is fully documented. There is no need for more discussion on this subject in this book.

- **Government coerced loans:**

    For over fifteen years, the Government has interfered in the home mortgage business forcing lenders to lower credit requirements. Lenders were induced to make loans to persons not capable of repaying those loans. This ill advised and little understood program is the cause of the economic crisis of 2008 and the home building boom that preceded it. This crisis was caused by the blatant use of implied government force to redistribute wealth from the lender to the borrower. However, it was the ordinary citizens, you, who were stuck with the bill and the misery it created. Wholesale destruction of wealth was the ultimate result. From the "WANNABE PEERS" point of view, this was a highly successful program that significantly increased poverty and the "WANNABE PEERS'" constituency.

There are many other programs similar to the ones mentioned above and the five programs that received the comprehensive analysis in chapters 7 through 11. There is no need to bore the reader with more specifics. If the people will embrace individual freedom, the violating programs will be identified and eliminated.

SUMMARY AND CONCLUSIONS:

This book has proven conclusively that the "WANNABE PEERS'" programs:

- DESTROY WEALTH
- INHIBIT THE CREATION OF WEALTH
- CREATE POVERTY AND MISERY FOR THE MASSES
- DESTROY INDIVIDUAL FREEDOM
- INCREASE THE "WANNABE PEERS'" CONSTITUENCY

The "WANNABE PEERS" claim that the only solution to problems created by their programs is more government regulations and surrender of more of our individual freedom. The "preponderance of propaganda" has convinced many "PAWNS" and pressure groups of the success of their programs. The illogical proposal that the only solution to problems created by the loss of our freedom is to surrender more of our freedom has received wide acceptance. The "WANNABE PEERS" are very close to creating the economic crisis that will create a totalitarian government in America or cause a revolution that will result in a totalitarian government. Just as an economic crisis brought tyrants to power in Italy and Germany, just as Cuba's revolution failed to restore freedom, the "WANNABE PEERS" can gain control of America. There will be no UNITED STATES left to save the world!

History has demonstrated that the "WANNABE PEERS" have used the power of the bureaucracy to prosecute and punish dissenters and there is no reason to believe that the current crop of "WANNABE PEERS" is any more moral than those of the past. Regaining our lost freedoms will be a dangerous undertaking, but the only alternative is the misery, abject poverty and mediocrity created by a totalitarian government. Just as the "MINUTEMEN" faced KING GEORGE III's English Regulars on Lexington Green, we are facing hoards of bureaucrats, backed by the "WANNABE PEERS". Will you stand up to the "WANNABE PEERS" as the "MINUTEMEN" stood up to KING GEORGE III or will you sink into the mediocrity of a totalitarian world?

IS THIS STILL THE "HOME OF THE BRAVE"?

THE END!

OR IS IT A NEW BEGINNING?
IT IS UP TO YOU!

GOD BLESS AMERICA

BIBLIOGRAPHY

1 Wikipedia Encyclopedia, Prohibition in the United States - http://en.wikipedia.org/wiki/Prohibition_in_the_United_States

2 Wikipedia encyclopedia http://en.wikipedia.org/wiki/Erie_Canal#Proposal_and_logistics

3 Ayn Rand's philosophy www.aynrand.org

4 Wikipedia encyclopedia List of countries by GDP (nominal)
     http://en.wikipedia.org/wiki/List_of_countries_by_GDP_(nominal

5 MEASURING WORTH U. S. GROSS DOMESTIC PRODUCT . http://www.measuringworth.org/usgdp/

6 "CLIMATE CONFUSION" Roy W. Spencer, ENCOUNTER BOOKS, NEW YORK

7 COMMONSENSE21C.COM - climate change page http://commonsense21c.com/CLIMATE.html

8 G.I.BILL http://en.wikipedia.org/wiki/G._I._Bill#After_World_War_II

9 PROMETHEUS http://en.wikipedia.org/wiki/Prometheus

10 INDUSTRIAL REVOLUTION Wikipedia encyclopedia

BIBLIOGRAPHY

http://en.wikipedia.org/wiki/Industrial_Revolu
tion/history

11 STEAM ENGINE Wikipedia encyclopedia
http://en.wikipedia.org/wiki/Steam_engine#Hist
ory

12 Wikipedia encyclopedia early
government charity Tenth Century
http://en.wikipedia.org/wiki/Almshouse

13 Wikipedia encyclopedia – quote from
JOHN DALBERG
http://en.wikipedia.org/wiki/John_Dalberg-
Acton,_1st_Baron_Acton#.22Lord_Acton.27s_dictu
m.22

14 Quote attributed to George Santayana
(1863?-1952), U.S. philosopher, poet.
http://plato.stanford.edu/entries/santayana/
Center for the Study of Language and
Information, Stanford University,
Stanford, CA 94305

15 Benito Amilcare Andrea Mussolini
Wikipedia Encyclopedia
http://en.wikipedia.org/wiki/Mussolini
MACROHISTORY AND WORLD REPORT
http://www.fsmitha.com/h2/ch12.htmhttp://gi.gr
olier.com/wwii/wwii_mussolini.html
http://www.newworldencyclopedia.org/entry/Beni
to_Mussolini#Early_Years

16 Adolf Hitler, The Life of Adolf
Hitler http://www.adolfhitler.dk/
http://en.wikipedia.org/wiki/Hitler
MACROHISTORY AND WORLD REPORT
http://www.fsmitha.com/h2/ch13.htm

http://www.fsmitha.com/h2/ch16.htm

http://www.fsmitha.com/h2/ch21b.html
        Sturmabteilung

http://en.wikipedia.org/wiki/Sturmabteilung
        SS or Schutzstaffel

http://encarta.msn.com/encyclopedia_761586855/SS.html
        "LIFE OF ADOLF HITLER"

http://www.adolfhitler.dk/
        NEW WORLD ENCYCLOPEDIA

http://www.newworldencyclopedia.org/entry/Hitler

        SPARTACUS EDUCATIONAL

http://www.spartacus.schoolnet.co.uk/GERsa.htm

        17 Fidel Alejandro Castro Ruz   Wikipedia Encyclopedia,

http://en.wikipedia.org/wiki/Fidel_Castro
Answers.com -

http://www.answers.com/topic/fidel-castro
MACROHISTORY AND WORLD REPORT

http://www.fsmitha.com/h2/ch24t63.html

        18 GEORGE WASHINGTON

http://encarta.msn.com/encyclopedia_761564084_7/George_Washington.html

        19 BENJAMIN FRANKLIN

http://www.wisdomquotes.com/000974.html

        20 JORDON, JOHN STEEL   "AN EMPIRE OF
WEALTH" NEW YORK,   HARPERCOLLINS PUBLISHERS
INC.

        21 MAGNA CARTA - Wikipedia encyclopedia

http://en.wikipedia.org/wiki/Magna_Carta

        22 SILVER CONTENT OF ROMAN COINS:

237

http://en.wikipedia.org/wiki/Roman_coinag
e#Further_history_of_Roman_coins

23 HISTORY OF METALWORKING:
http://www.bloodandsawdust.com/sca/lathes.html

24 SHERMAN ANTITRUST ACT:
http://everything2.com/index.pl?node_id=548896
http://en.wikipedia.org/wiki/Sherman_Anti_Trus
t_Act
http://topics.law.cornell.edu/wex/Antitrust
http://www.cato.org/pubs/journal/cj9n3/cj9n3-
13.pdf
http://www.cato.org/pubs/handbook/hb105-
39.html
http://en.wikipedia.org/wiki/Alan_Greenspan
http://www.fsmitha.com/h3/h46-am.htm

25 LEXINGTON GREEN
http://en.wikipedia.org/wiki/Lexington_Green
http://www.newworldencyclopedia.org/entry/Batt
les_of_Lexington_and_Concord

26 CONSTITUTIONAL CONVENTION
http://en.wikipedia.org/wiki/Philadelphia_Conv
ention
http://en.wikipedia.org/wiki/Timeline_of_the_U
nited_States_Constitution

27 MANIFEST DESTINY
http://en.wikipedia.org/wiki/Manifest_Destiny
http://www.newworldencyclopedia.org/entry/Mani
fest_Destiny

28 SUFFRAGE
http://en.wikipedia.org/wiki/Voting_and_electi
ons

29 PROPAGANDA
http://www.newworldencyclopedia.org/entry/Prop
aganda

30 THE DIVINE RIGHT OF KINGS
http://www.newworldencyclopedia.org/entry/Divi
ne_right_of_kings

31 PATRICK HENRY
http://en.wikipedia.org/wiki/Patrick_Henry

32 RONALD REAGAN
http://en.wikipedia.org/wiki/Ronald_Reagan

33 STANDARD OIL:
    http://www.bookrags.com/wiki/Standard_Oil
http://en.wikipedia.org/wiki/Standard_Oil
http://en.citizendium.org/wiki/Standard_Oil
http://www.reference.com/browse/Standard+Oil+C
ompany?jss=1
http://www.theobjectivestandard.com/issues/200
8-summer/standard-oil-company.asp
http://books.google.com/books?id=aIIEAAAAMAAJ&
pg=PA1&dq=intitle:standard+intitle:oil&num=30&
as_brr=1#PPA1,M1

34 NOTHERN SECURITIES COMPANY ANTITRUST
http://en.wikipedia.org/wiki/Northern_Securiti
es_Company
35 "FDR and the IRS" by Burton W.
Folsom, Jr. Prepared for the Durell
Colloquium," The Role of Markets and
Governments in Pursuing the Common Good," at
Hillsdale College, October 28, 2006.

36 Sbardellati, John.
*Power to Destroy: The Political Uses of the
IRS from Kennedy to Nixon*

37 "The Lawless State: The Crimes of the
U. S. Intelligence Agencies" by Morton H.
Halperin (Author), Jerry J. Berman (Author),
Robert L. Borosage (Author), Christine M.
Marwick

38 HYPERINFLATION:
http://www.newworldencyclopedia.org/entry/Weim
ar_Republic
http://en.wikipedia.org/wiki/Hyperinflation

39 DODO BIRD:
http://en.wikipedia.org/wiki/Dodo_(bird)

40 "THE ENABLING ACT OF 1933":
http://en.wikipedia.org/wiki/Enabling_Act_(Ger
many)

41 IRA TARBELL
http://en.wikipedia.org/wiki/Ida_Tarbell
http://www.bookrags.com/biography/ida-minerva-
tarbell/
    "THE HISTORY OF THE STANDARD OIL COMPANY"
(New York, NY: McClure, Philips & Company
1904) pp. 36-37
42 ECONOMY OF SCALE:
http://en.wikipedia.org/wiki/Economy_of_scale

43 JOHN D. ROCKEFELLER:
http://en.wikipedia.org/wiki/John_D._Rockefell
er
http://www.bgsu.edu/departments/acs/1890s/rock
efeller/bio2.htm
http://en.wikipedia.org/wiki/Allan_Nevins

44 ROBBER BARONS:
http://en.wikipedia.org/wiki/Robber_baron_(ind
ustrialist)

45 ALLEN NEVINS
http://en.wikipedia.org/wiki/Allan_Nevins

46 INFLATION RATE 1914-PRESENT:
http://inflationdata.com/Inflation/Inflation_R
ate/HistoricalInflation.aspx

47 THOMAS PAINE:
http://en.wikipedia.org/wiki/Thomas_Paine%27s_
Common_Sense

48 INTERSTATE COMMERCE COMMISSION:
http://en.wikipedia.org/wiki/Interstate_Commer
ce_Commission
http://en.wikipedia.org/wiki/Regulatory_captur
e
http://www.pbs.org/wgbh/amex/streamliners/peop
leevents/e_ica.html
JORDON, JOHN STEEL *"AN EMPIRE OF WEALTH"*
NEW YORK, HARPERCOLLINS PUBLISHERS INC.
http://encarta.msn.com/encyclopedia_76157
2204/Government_Regulation_of_Railroads.html
http://www.american-
rails.com/railroading-in-the-1930s.html
http://www.history.com/encyclopedia.do?article
Id=220264
http://www.aar.org/PubCommon/Documents/AboutTh
eIndustry/Overview.pdf

49 GOVERNMENT FAILURE
http://en.wikipedia.org/wiki/Government_failur
e

50 "IRON TRIANGLE"
http://en.wikipedia.org/wiki/Iron_triangle
http://www.auburn.edu/~johnspm/gloss/iron_tria
ngles

51 GOVERNMENT AGENCYS
http://en.wikipedia.org/wiki/Independent_agenc
ies_of_the_United_States_government

52 WOODROW WILSON - The New Freedom: A
Call For the Emancipation of the Generous
Energies of a People - PUBLISHER BIBLIOBAZAAR

53 "REGULATORY CAPTURE"
http://en.wikipedia.org/wiki/Regulatory_captur
e
54 EARMARKS:
http://en.wikipedia.org/wiki/Earmark_(politics
)
http://earmarks.omb.gov/2008_appropriatio
ns_earmarks_110th_congress.html
http://www.measuringworth.org/usgdp/
http://en.wikipedia.org/wiki/U.S._population

55 inflation calculator:
http://www.westegg.com/inflation/
http://www.halfhill.com/inflation.html
http://www.moneychimp.com/articles/econ/inflat
ion_calculator.htm
http://www.bls.gov/data/inflation_calculator.h
tm

56 OVERVIEW OF AMERICA'S FREIGHT
RAILROADS
http://www.aar.org/PubCommon/Documents/AboutTh
eIndustry/Overview.pdf

57 FEDERAL RESERVE SYSTEM:
http://www.federalreserve.gov/aboutthefed/defa
ult.htm
    http://www.federalreserveeducation.org/fe
d101/history/
http://en.wikipedia.org/wiki/Federal_Reserve_S
ystem

58 PRICE OF GOLD
http://www.finfacts.ie/Private/curency/goldmar
ketprice.htm

59 PRICE OF SILVER
http://www.goldmastersusa.com/silver_historica
l_prices.asp

60 GREENBACK:
http://ecclesia.org/forum/uploads/bondservant/
greenbackP.pdf

61 INFLATION DATA:
http://inflationdata.com/inflation/Inflation_R
ate/HistoricalInflation.aspx?dsInflation_curre
ntPage=7
http://www.nowandfutures.com/key_stats.html

62 INFLATION:
http://wordnetweb.princeton.edu/perl/webwn?s=i
nflation

63 INCOME TAX
http://en.wikipedia.org/wiki/History_of_Income
_Taxation_in_the_United_States#Income_tax
http://www.ntu.org/main/page.php?PageID=19

64 COMPLEXITY AND COST OF TAX CODE
http://74.125.47.132/search?q=cache:MgroUVPv3W
4J:www.taxfoundation.org/files/sr138.pdf+cost+

of+complying+with+coperate+income+tax&cd=1&hl=
en&ct=clnk&gl=us

    65 TESTIMONY OF DAVID BURNHAM ON IRS
ABUSES (testimony before a Senate committee)
http://famguardian.org/TaxFreedom/Evidence/Con
gressional/DavidBurnhamTestimony.htm

    66 Lyndon Johnson, the IRS and churches
http://www.gather.com/viewArticle.action?artic
leId=281474977666190

    67   PERCENT OF POPULATION WORKING IN
AGRICULTURE
http://www.ers.usda.gov/publications/eib3/eib3
.htm

    68 WANNABE PEERS USE OF THE IRS 1977-
PRESENT
http://www.wnd.com/news/article.asp?ARTICLE_ID
=14702
http://www.papillonsartpalace.com/churches.htm
http://www.judicialwatch.org/printer_2371.shtm
l http://www.judicialwatch.org/1737.shtml
http://www.fieldwerks.com/bush.htm
http://www.democraticunderground.com/discuss/d
uboard.php?az=view_all&address=110x10771
http://eatatjoesplace.blogspot.com/2005/11/pre
sident-bushs-war-on-people-of-faith.html

    69 IRS REFORM 1998
http://www.washingtonpost.com/wp-
srv/politics/special/tax/stories/irs072398.htm

    70 CLINTON'S ENEMIES AND THE IRS
http://archive.newsmax.com/archives/articles/2
002/4/22/200136.shtml

71 VICTIMLESS CRIMES - LIBRARY OF HALEXANDRIA:
http://www.halexandria.org/dward267.htm
"AIN'T NOBODY'S BUSINESS IF YOU DO" book by Peter McWilliams

72 MARIJUANA - % OF U.S. AGRICULTURAL GDP
http://www.drugscience.org/Archive/bcr2/cashcr ops.html

LaVergne, TN USA
05 November 2009

163114LV00002B/48/P